THE BIG BOOK OF Christmas Carols

ISBN. 978-0-7119-8992-3

Visit Hal Leonard Online at
www.halleonard.com

Contact us:
Hal Leonard
7777 West Bluemound Road
Milwaukee, WI 53213
Email: info@halleonard.com

In Europe, contact:
Hal Leonard Europe Limited
42 Wigmore Street
Marylebone, London, W1U 2RY
Email: info@halleonardeurope.com

In Australia, contact:
Hal Leonard Australia Pty. Ltd.
4 Lentara Court
Cheltenham, Victoria, 3192 Australia
Email: info@halleonard.com.au

A Child This Day Is Born

Traditional

Verse 2:
These tidings shepherds heard
In field watching their fold
Were by an angel unto them
That night reveal'd and told:

Nowell, Nowell, *etc.*

Verse 3:
To whom the angel spoke
Saying "Be not afraid"
Be glad, poor silly shepherds
Why are you so dismayed?"

Nowell, Nowell, *etc.*

Verse 4:
"For lo! I bring you tidings
Of gladness and of mirth
Which cometh to all people by
This holy infant's birth":

Nowell, Nowell, *etc.*

Verse 5:
Then was there with the angel
An host incontinent
Of heavenly bright soldiers
Which from the Highest was sent:

Nowell, Nowell, *etc.*

Verse 6:
Lauding the Lord our God
And his celestial King
All glory be in paradise
This heav'nly host did sing:

Nowell, Nowell, *etc.*

Verse 7:
And as the angel told them
So to them did appear
They found the young child Jesus Christ
With Mary, his mother dear:

Nowell, Nowell, *etc.*

All Through The Night

Traditional

Andante

G C A7 D

Sleep my love, and peace at - tend thee

C Am7 D D7 G C

all through the night. Guard - ian an - gels,

A7 D C Am7 D D7 G

God will lead thee all through the night.

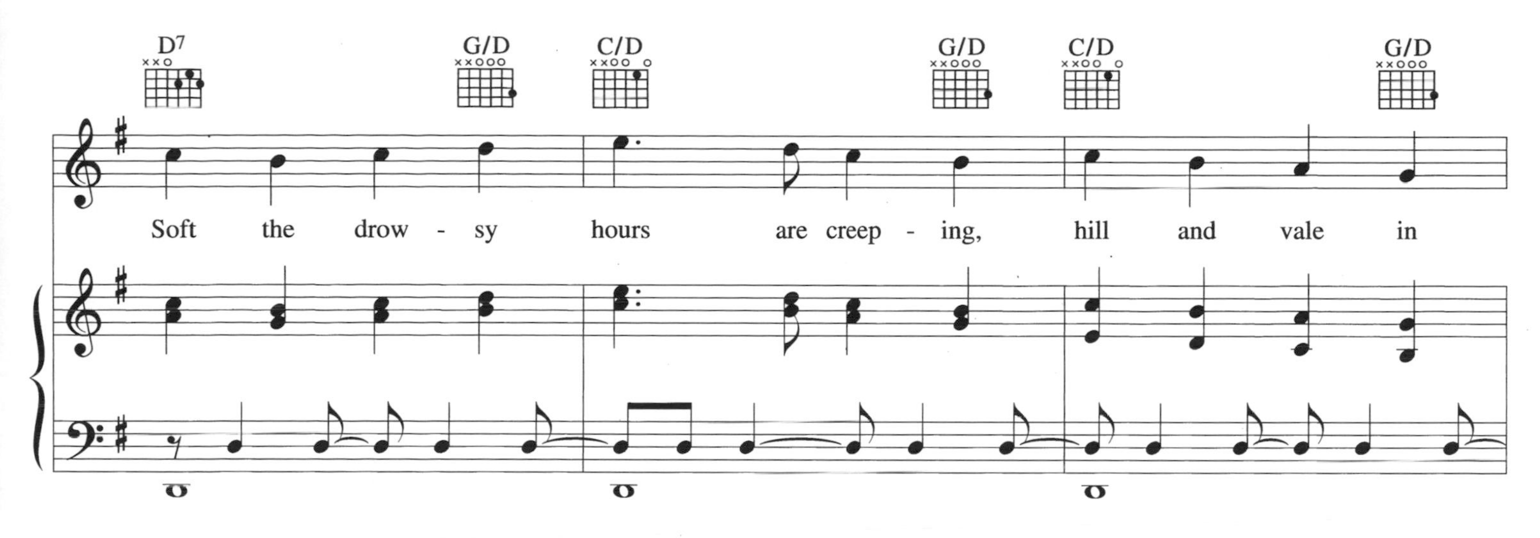
D7
G/D
C/D
G/D
C/D
G/D
Soft the drow - sy hours are creep - ing, hill and vale in

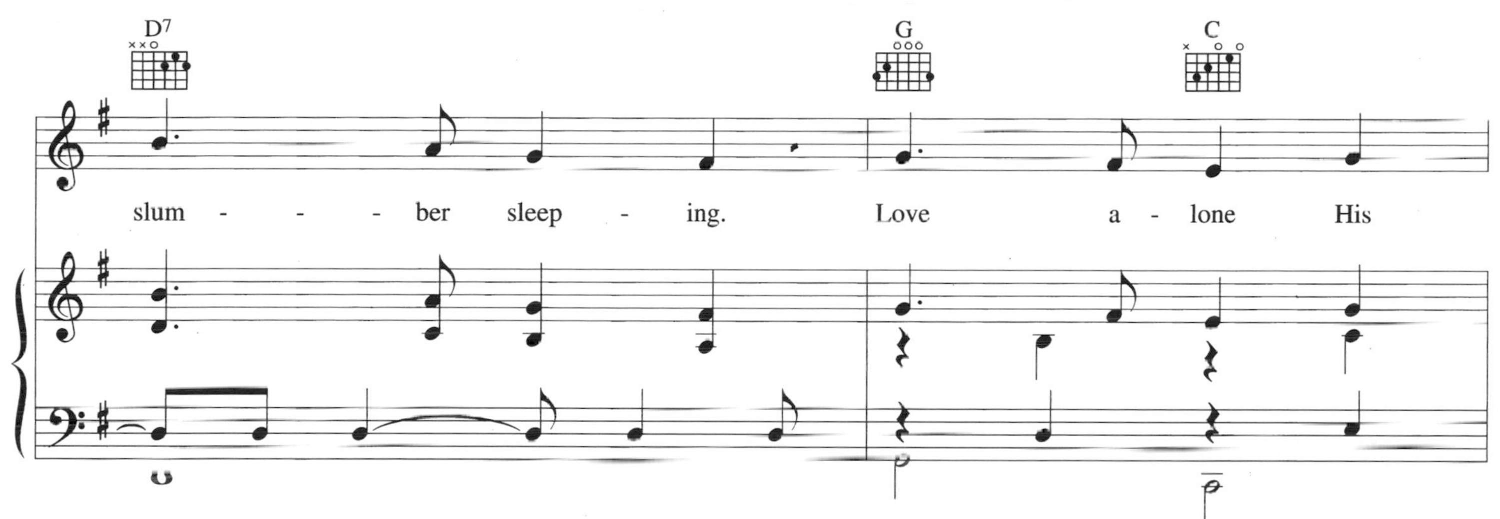
D7
G
C
slum - - - ber sleep - ing. Love a - lone His

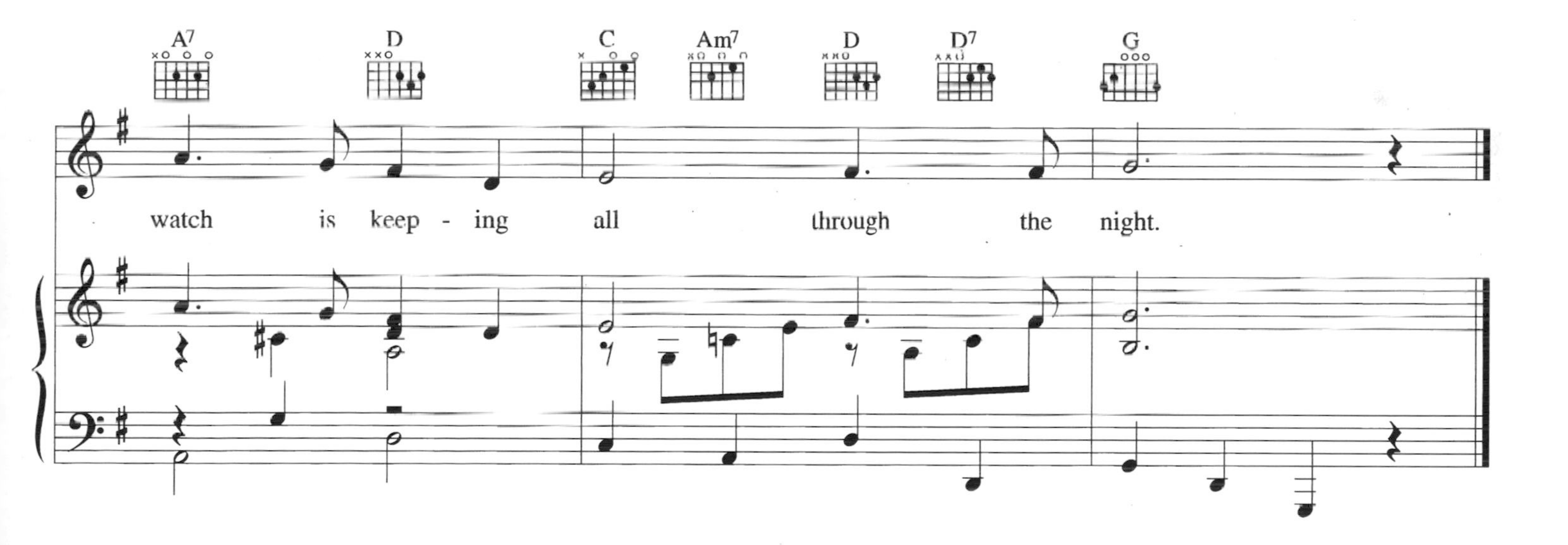
A7
D
C
Am7
D
D7
G
watch is keep - ing all through the night.

Angels From The Realms Of Glory

Music: Traditional
Words by James Montgomery

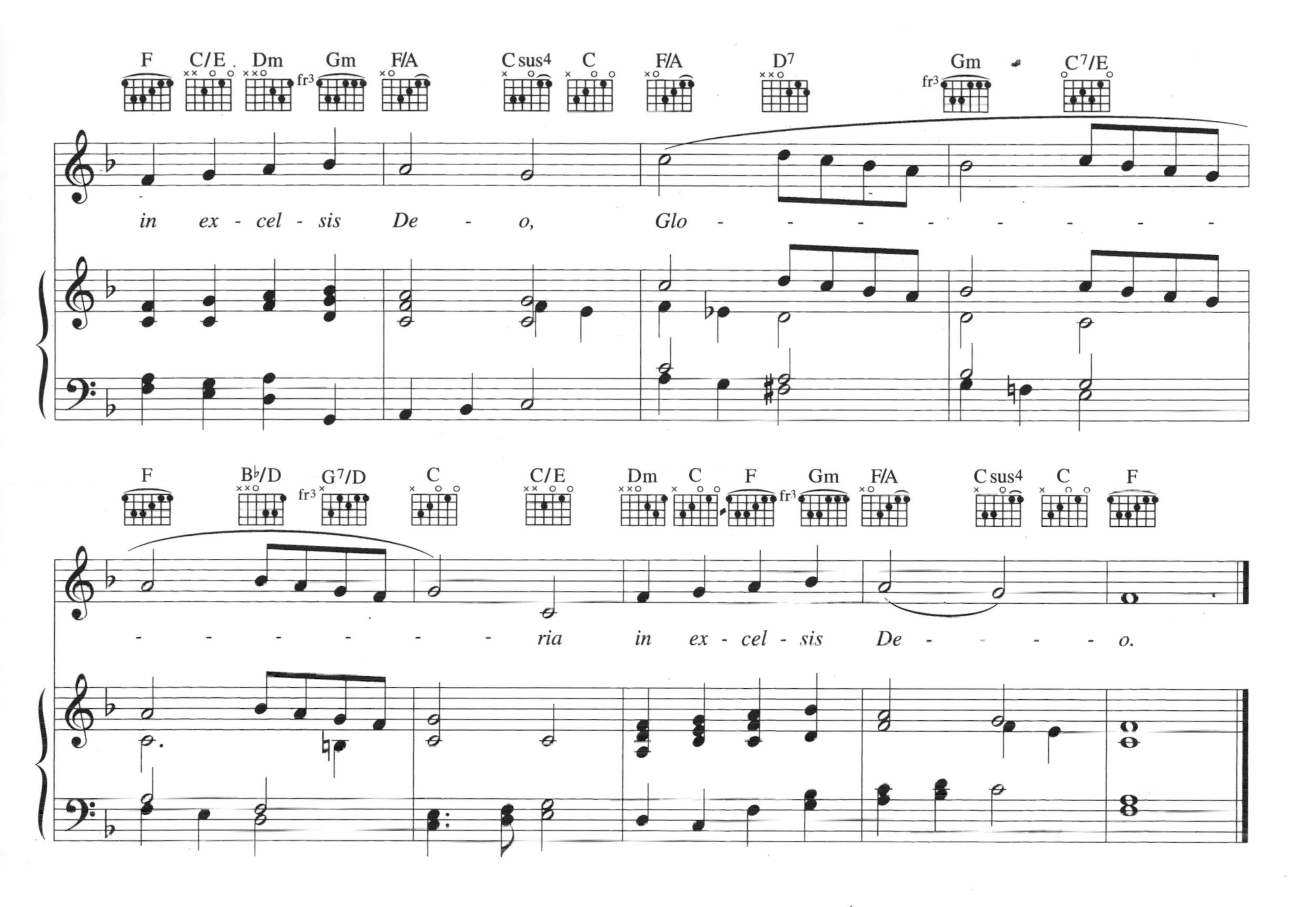

Verse 2:
Shepherds in the field abiding
Watching o'er your flocks by night
God with man is now residing
Yonder shines the infant Light.

Gloria in excelsis Deo
Gloria in excelsis Deo.

Verse 3:
Sages, leave your comtemplations
Brighter visions beam afar
Seek the great Desire of Nations
Ye have seen his natal star.

Gloria in excelsis Deo
Gloria in excelsis Deo.

Verse 4:
Saints before the altar bending
Watching long in hope and fear
Suddenly the Lord, descending
In his temple shall appear.

Gloria in excelsis Deo
Gloria in excelsis Deo.

Verse 5:
Though an infant now we view him
He shall fill his Father's throne
Gather all the nations to him
Every knee shall then bow down.

Gloria in excelsis Deo
Gloria in excelsis Deo.

As With Gladness Men Of Old

Words by William Chatterton Dix
Music by Conrad Kocher

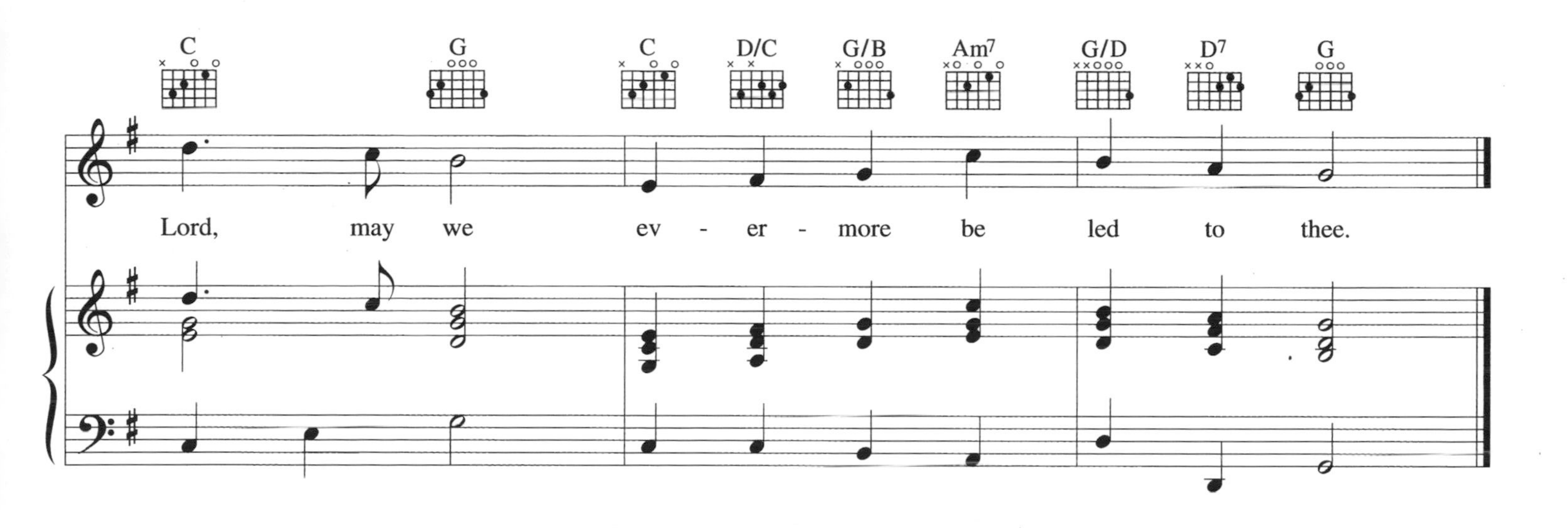

Verse 2:
As with joyful steps they sped
To that lowly manger-bed
There to bend the knee before
Him whom heav'n and earth adore
So may we with willing feet
Ever seek thy mercy-seat.

Verse 3:
As their precious gifts they laid
At thy manger roughly made
So may we with holy joy
Pure, and free from sin's alloy
All our costliest treasures bring
Christ, to thee, our heav'nly King.

Verse 4:
Holy Jesu, ev'ry day
Keep us in the narrow way;
And, when earthly things are past,
Bring our ransomed souls at last
Where they need no star to guide,
Where no clouds thy glory hide.

Verse 5:
In the heav'nly country bright
Need they no created light;
Thou its light, its joy, its crown,
Thou its sun which goes not down;
There for ever may we sing
Alleluias to our King.

Auld Lang Syne

Music: Traditional
Words by Robert Burns

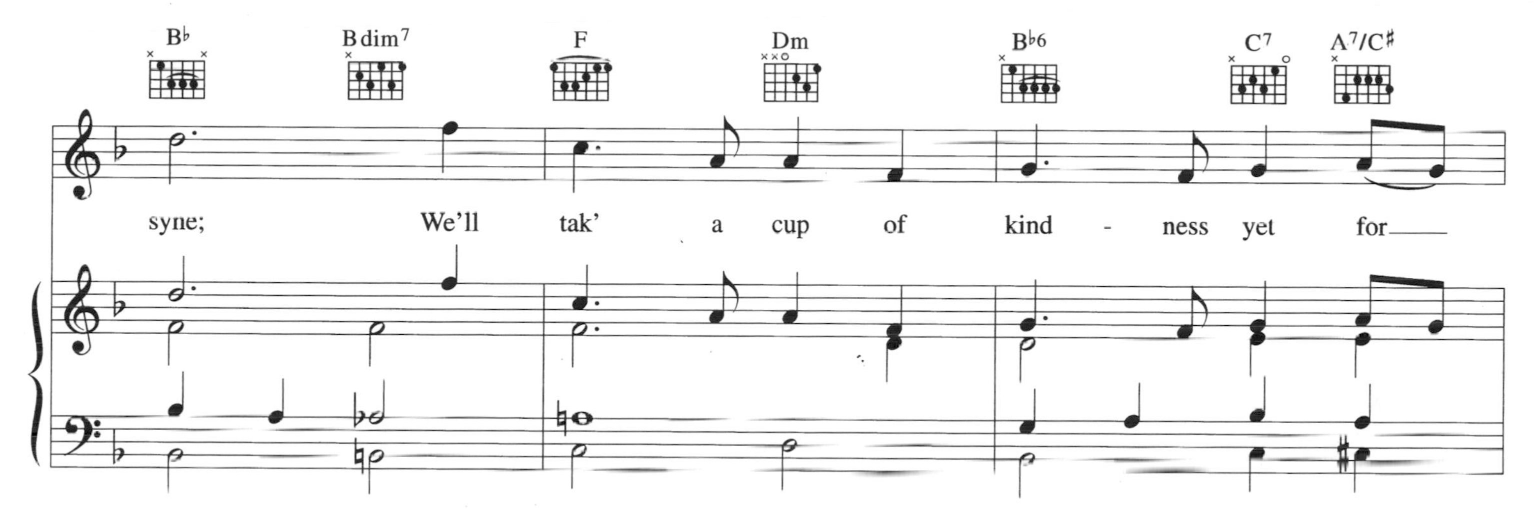

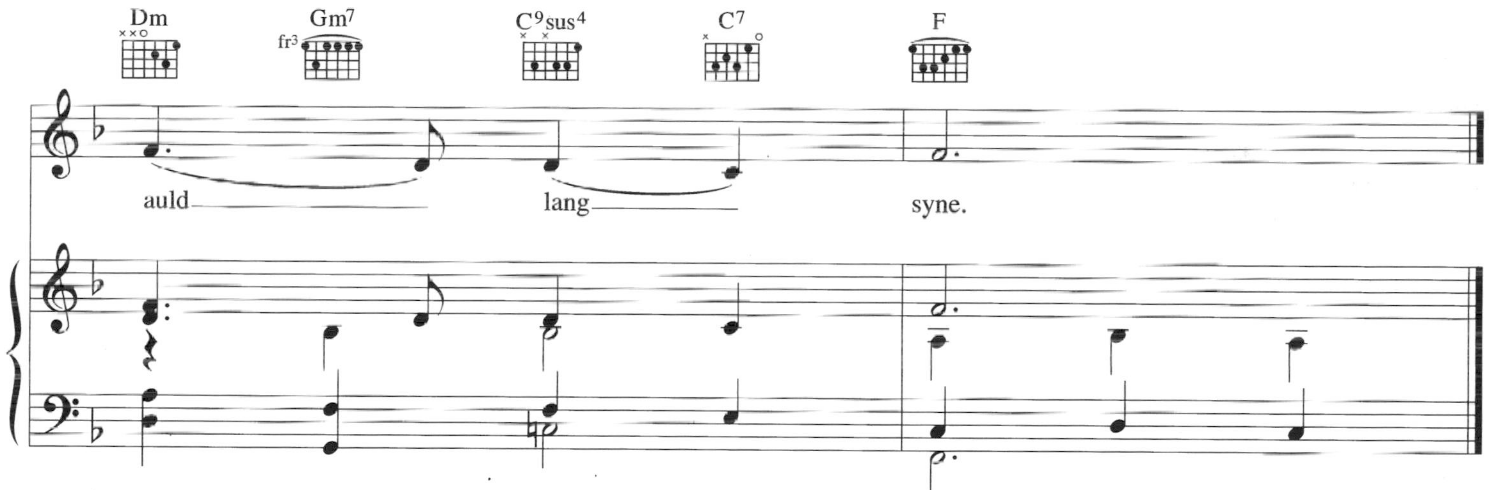

Verse 2:
And here's a hand, my trusty frien'
And gie's a hand o' thine?
We'll tak' a cup o' kindness yet
For auld lang syne?

For auld lang syne *etc.*

Away In A Manger

Words: Traditional
Music by William Kirkpatrick

2. The cattle are lowing
The baby awakes
But little Lord Jesus
No crying He makes
I Love thee, Lord Jesus!
Look down from the sky
And stay by my side
Until morning is nigh

3. Be near me, Lord Jesus
I ask thee to stay
Close by me forever
And love me, I pray
Bless all the dear children
In Thy tender care
And fit us for heaven
To live with Thee there.

The Boar's Head Carol

Traditional

Verse 2:
The boar's head, as I understand
Is the rarest dish in all this land
Which thus bedecked with a gay garland
Let us *servire cantico*
Caput apri defero
Reddens laudes Domino.

Verse 3:
Our steward hath provided this
In honour of the King of bliss
Which on this day to be served is
In Reginensi atrio
Caput apri defero
Reddens laudes Domino.

The Coventry Carol

Traditional

Verse 2:
Herod, the king, in his raging
Chargèd he hath this day.
His men of might, in his own sight
All young children to slay.

Verse 3:
That woe is me, poor child for thee!
And ever morn and day.
For thy parting, neither say nor sing
By by, lully lullay!

Deck The Halls

Traditional

2. See the blazing Yule before us
Fa-la-la-la-la, la-la-la-la
Strike the harp and join the chorus
Fa-la-la-la-la, la-la-la-la
Follow me in merry measure
Fa-la-la, la-la-la, la-la-la
While I tell of Yuletide treasure
Fa-la-la-la-la, la-la-la-la.

3. Fast away the old year passes
Fa-la-la-la-la, la-la-la-la
Hail the new, ye lads and lasses
Fa-la-la-la-la, la-la-la-la
Sing we joyous all together
Fa-la-la, la-la-la, la-la-la
Heedless of the wind and weather
Fa-la-la-la-la, la-la-la-la.

Ding Dong Merrily On High

Music: Traditional
Words by George Woodward

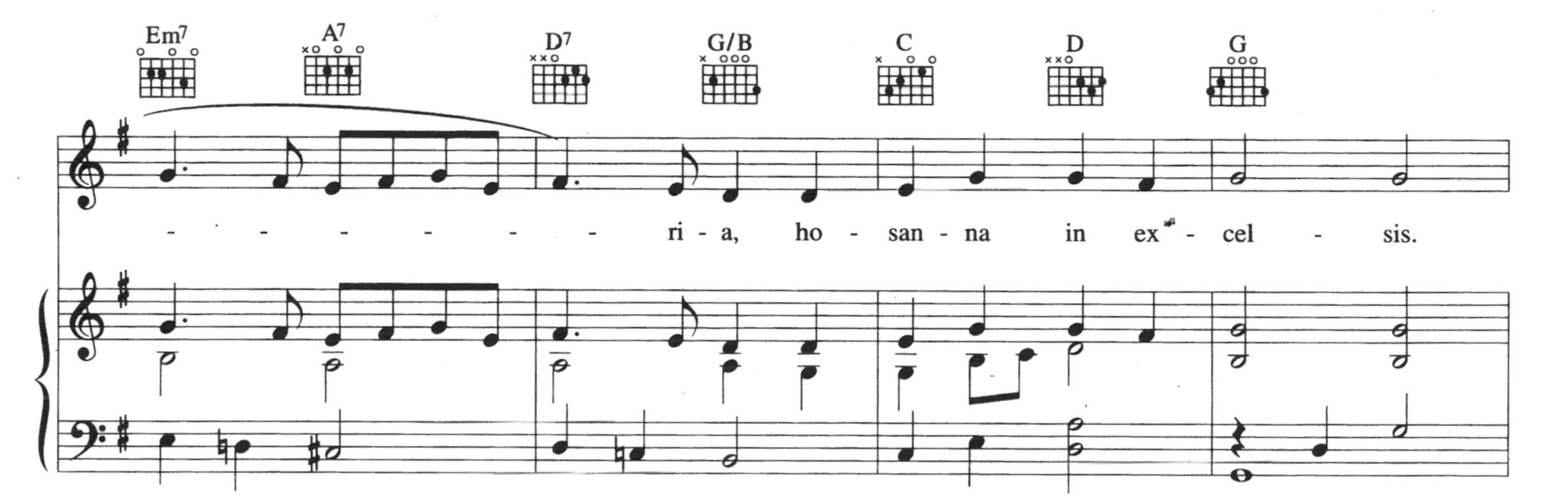

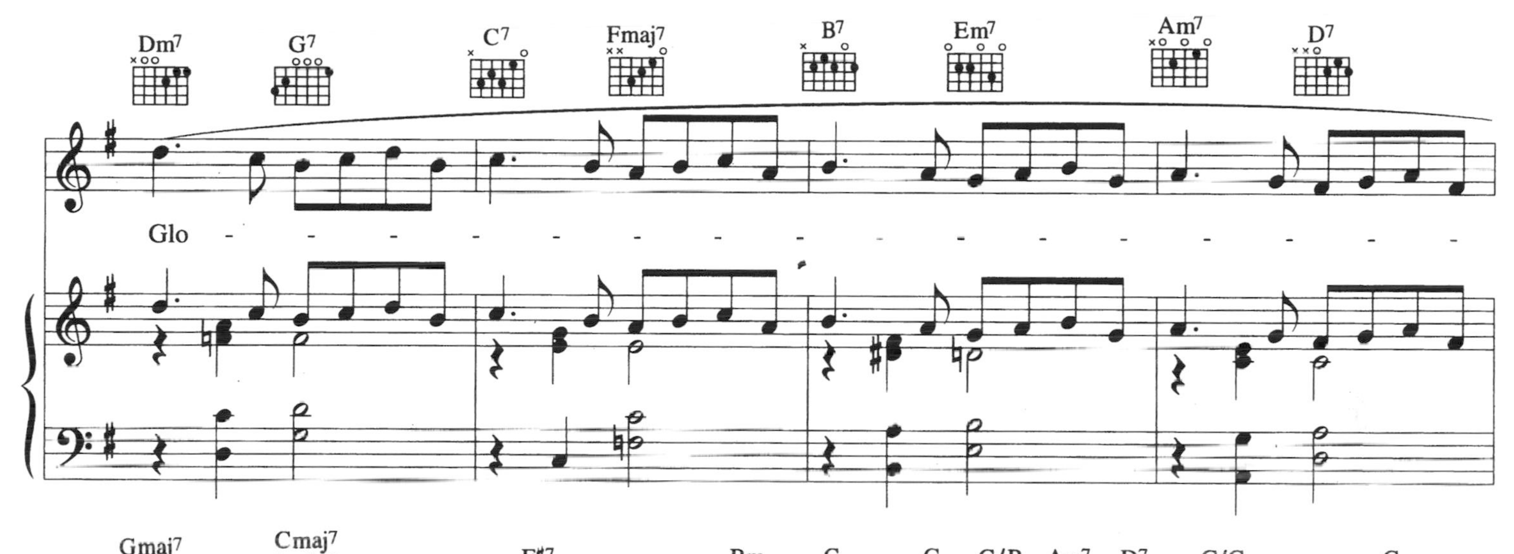

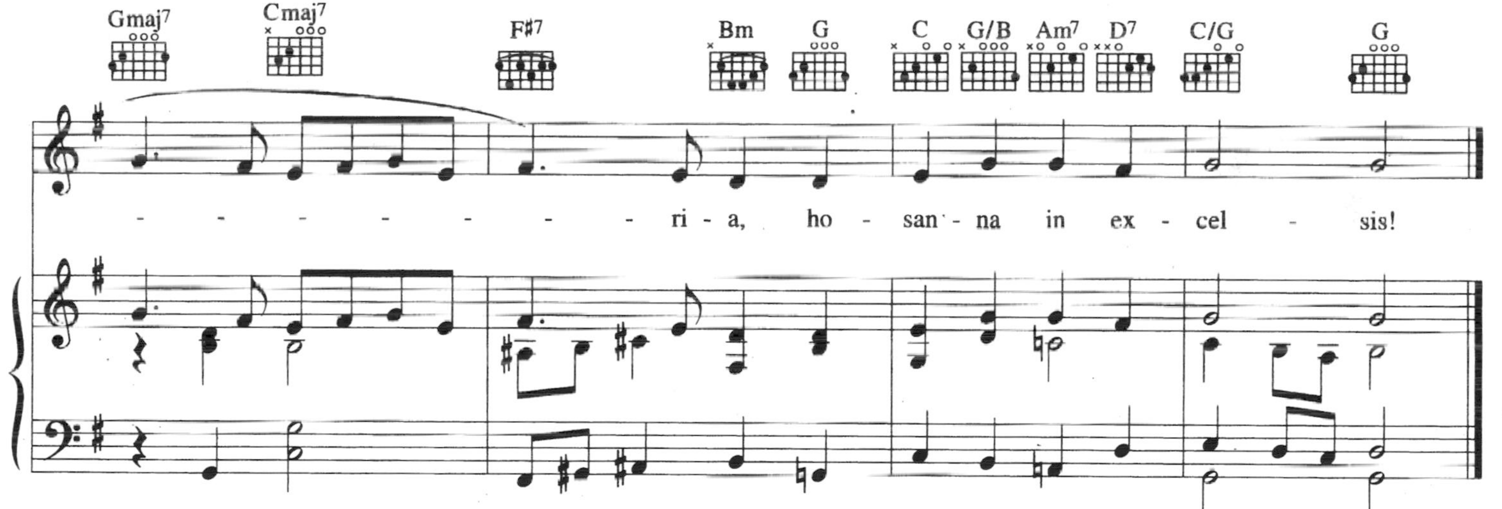

Verse 2:
E'en so, here below, below
Let steeple bells be swungen
And i-o, i-o, i-o
By priest and people sungen!

Gloria, hosanna in excelsis
Gloria, hosanna in excelsis!

Verse 3:
Pray you, dutifully prime
Your matin chime, you ringers
May you beautifully rhyme
Your evetime song, you singers.

Gloria, hosanna in excelsis
Gloria, hosanna in excelsis!

The First Nowell

Traditional

2. They looked up and saw a star
   Shining in the east beyond them far
   And to the earth it gave great light
   And so it continued both day and night.
   Refrain

3. This star drew nigh to the northwest
   O'er Bethlehem it took its rest
   And there it did both stop and stay
   Right over the place where Jesus lay.
   Refrain

4. Then entered in those wisemen three
   Full rev'rently upon their knee
   And offered there in His presence
   Their gold and myrrh and frankincense.
   Refrain

God Rest Ye Merry, Gentlemen

Traditional

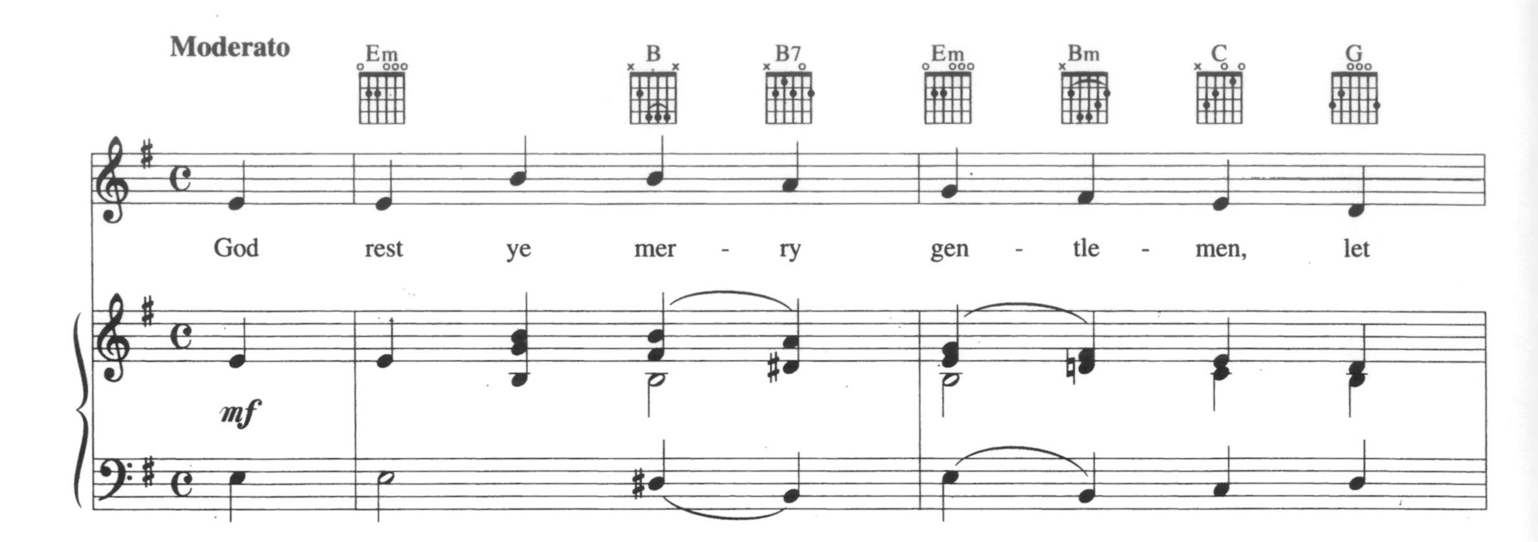

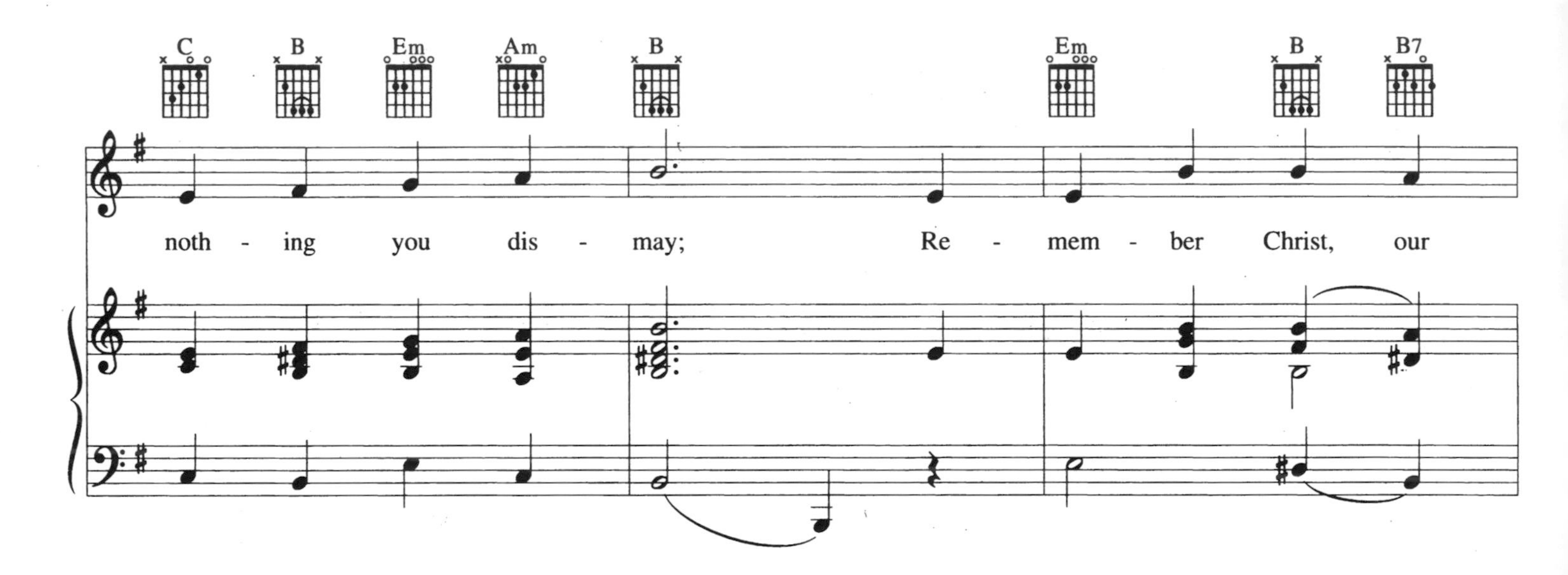

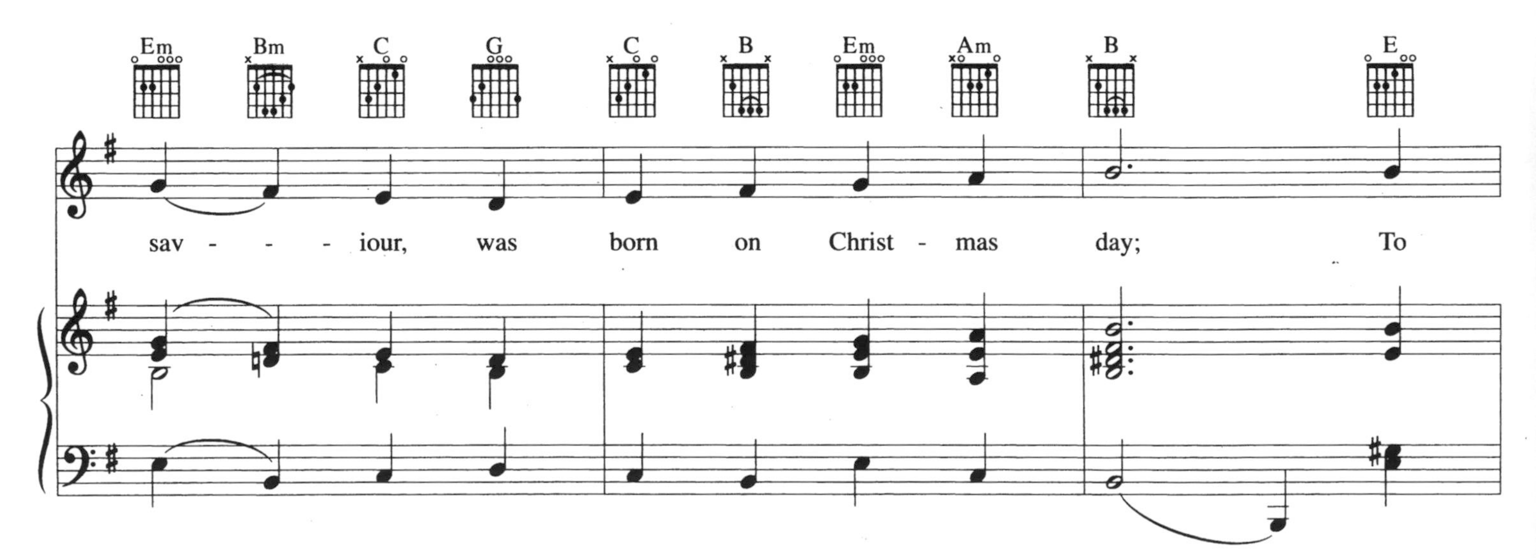

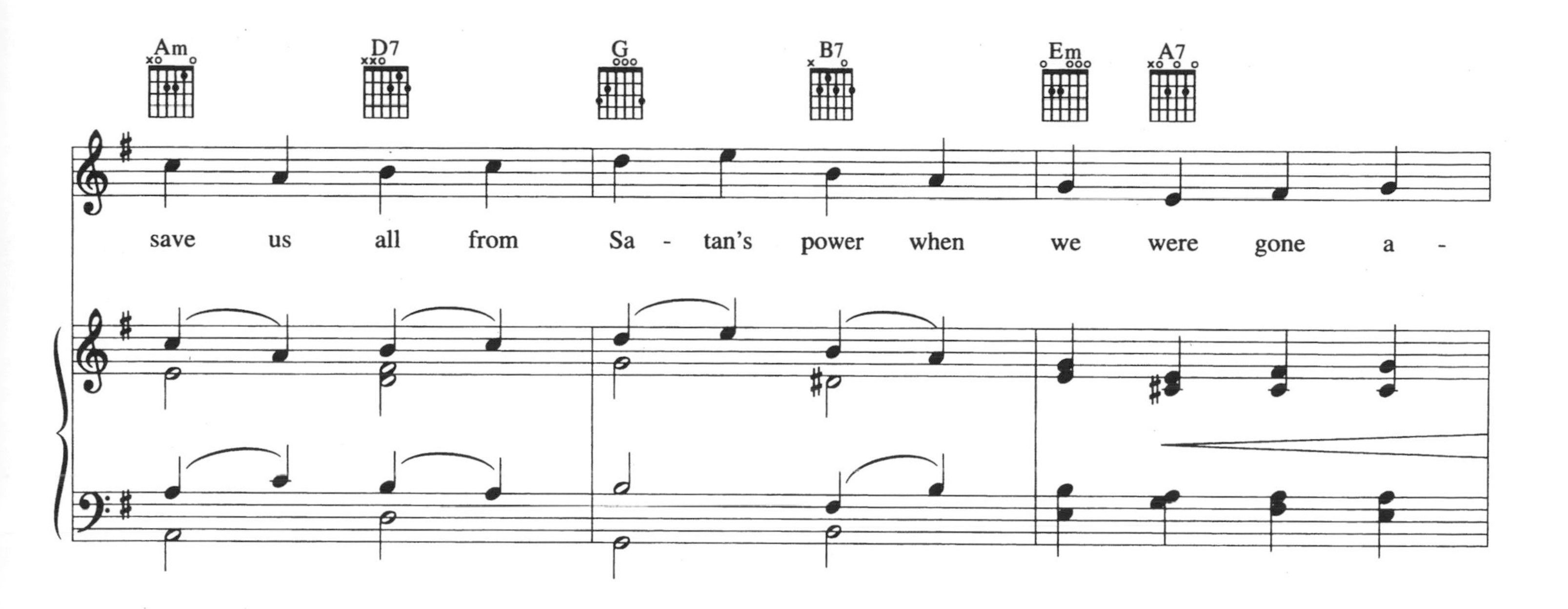
Am D7 G B7 Em A7
save us all from Sa - tan's power when we were gone a -

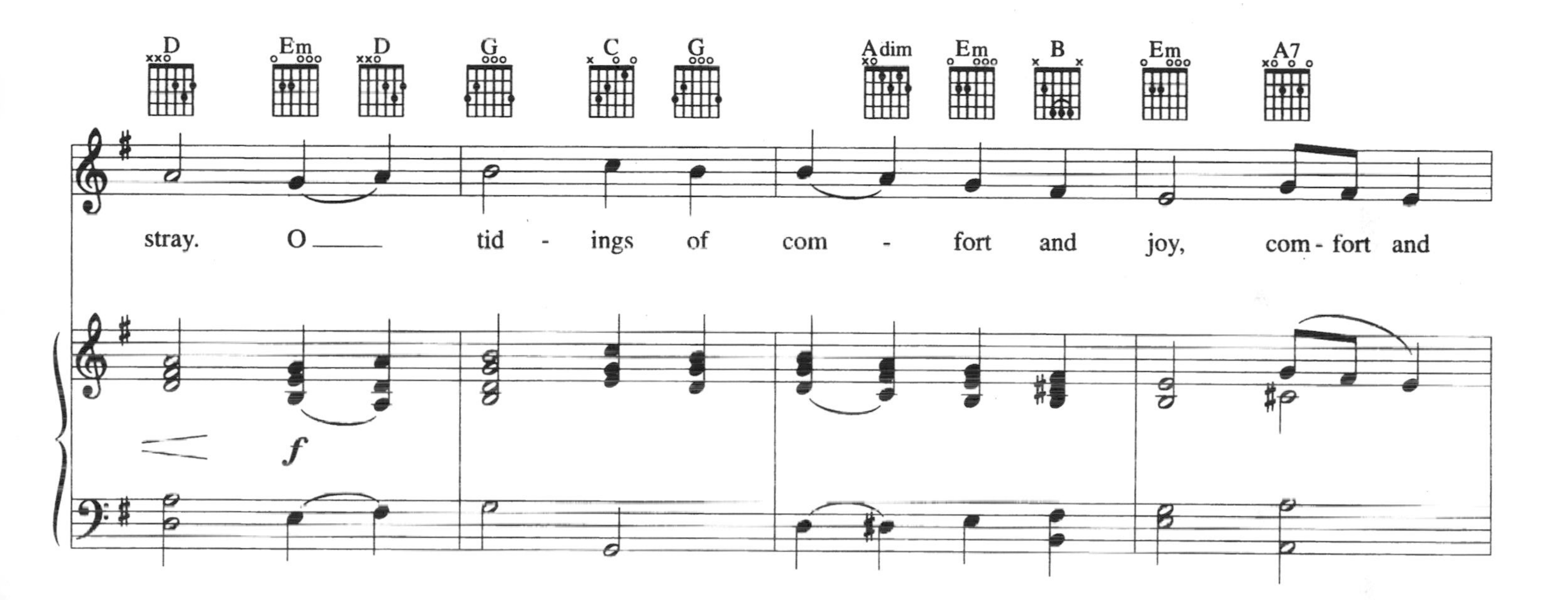
D Em D G C G Adim Em B Em A7
stray. O tid - ings of com - fort and joy, com - fort and
f

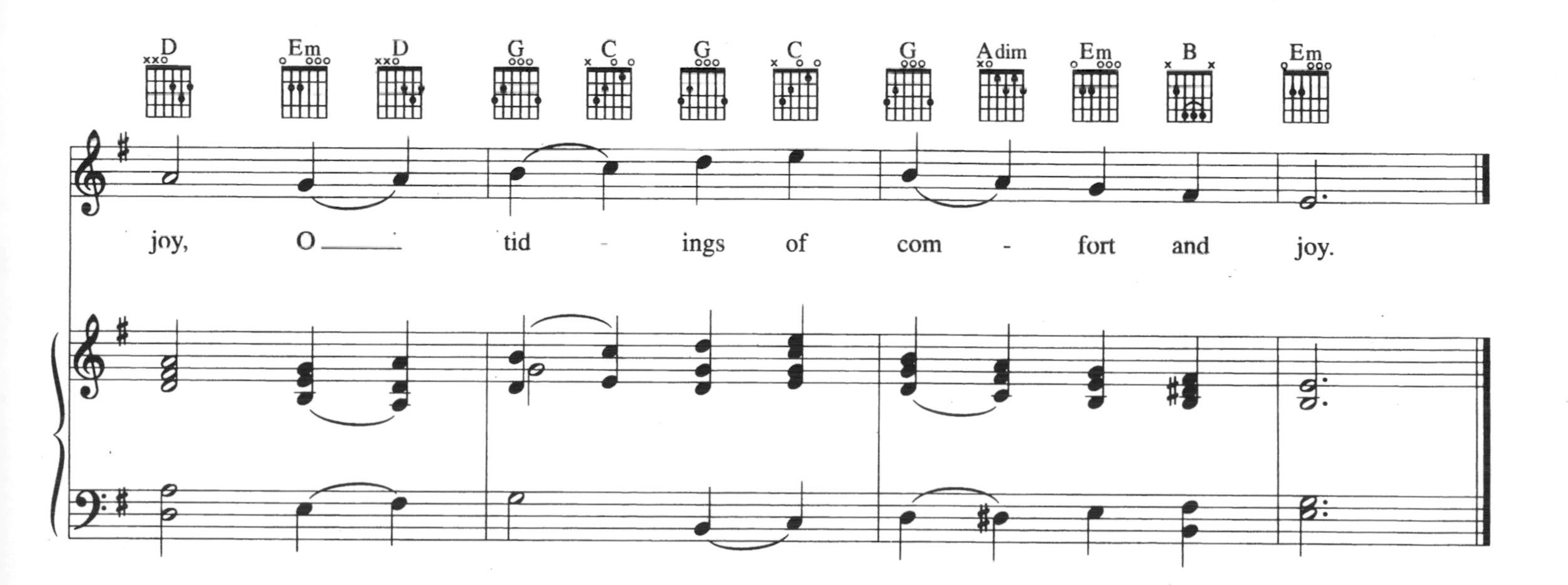
D Em D G C G C G Adim Em B Em
joy, O tid - ings of com - fort and joy.

Jingle Bells

Traditional

2.
C7
B♭/D
C/E
F
C7
ride and sing a sleigh - ing song to - night. Oh,
mf
F
Dm
C/E
jin - gle bells, jin - gle bells, jin - gle all the
L.H.
L.H.
F
Gm
fr3
C7
F
way, oh what fun it is to ride in a
1.
G7
C
C7
2.
C7
F
one horse o - pen sleigh.
one horse o - pen sleigh.

Good King Wenceslas

Music: Traditional
Words by John Neale

2. "Hither, page, and stand by me
If thou know'st it, telling
Yonder peasant who is he?
Where and what his dwelling?"
"Sire, he lives a good league hence
Underneath the mountain
Right against the forest fence
By St. Agnes fountain!"

3. "Bring me flesh and bring me wine
Bring me pine logs hither
Thou and I will see him dine
When we bear them hither"
Page and monarch forth they went
Forth they went together
Through the rude wind's wild lament
And the bitter weather.

Hark! The Herald Angels Sing

Music by Felix Mendelssohn
Words by Charles Wesley

2. Christ, by highest heaven adored
Christ the everlasting Lord
Come, Desire of Nations, come
Fix in us thy humble home
Veiled in flesh the Godhead see
Hail th'Incarnate Deity
Pleased as man with man to dwell
Jesus, our Emmanuel.
Refrain

3. Hail, the heavenborn Prince of Peace!
Hail, the Sun of Righteousness!
Light and life to all He brings,
Risen with healing in His wings
Mild He lays His glory by
Born that man no more may die
Born to raise the sons of earth
Born to give them second birth.
Refrain

The Holly And The Ivy

Traditional

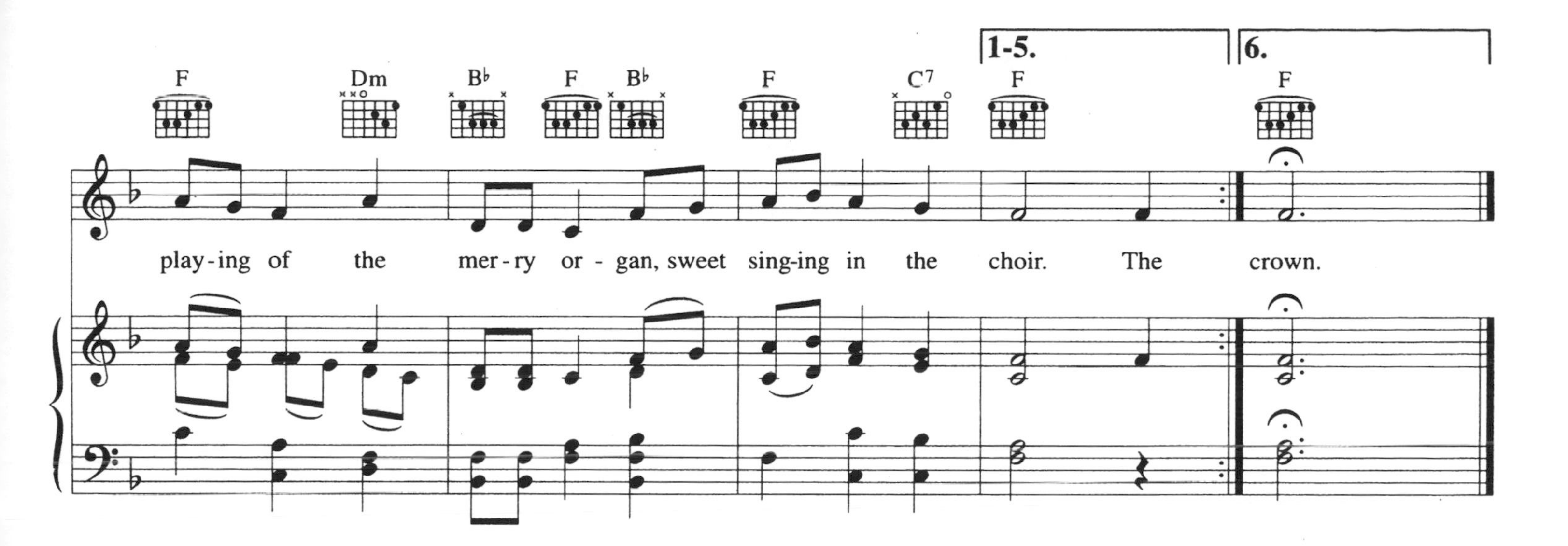

Verse 2:
The holly bears a blossom
As white as the flow'r
And Mary bore sweet Jesus Christ
To be our sweet saviour.

The rising of *etc.*

Verse 3:
The holly bears a berry
As red as any blood
And Mary bore sweet Jesus Christ
To do poor sinners good.

The rising of *etc.*

Verse 4:
The holly bears a prickle
As sharp as any thorn
And Mary bore sweet Jesus Christ
On Christmas Day in the morn.

The rising of *etc.*

Verse 5:
The holly bears a bark
As bitter as any gall
And Mary bore sweet Jesus Christ
For to redeem us all.

The rising of *etc.*

Verse 6:
The holly and the ivy
When they are both full grown
Of all the trees that are in the wood
The holly bears the crown.

The rising of *etc.*

How Far Is It To Bethlehem?

Traditional

Verse 3:
May we stroke the creatures there
Ox, ass, or sheep?
May we peep like them and see
Jesus asleep?

Verse 4:
If we touch his tiny hand
Will he awake?
Will he know we've come so far
Just for his sake?

Verse 5:
Great kings have precious gifts
And we have naught
Little smiles and little tears
Are all we brought.

Verse 6:
For all weary children
Mary must weep
Here, on his bed of straw
Sleep, children sleep.

I Saw Three Ships

Traditional

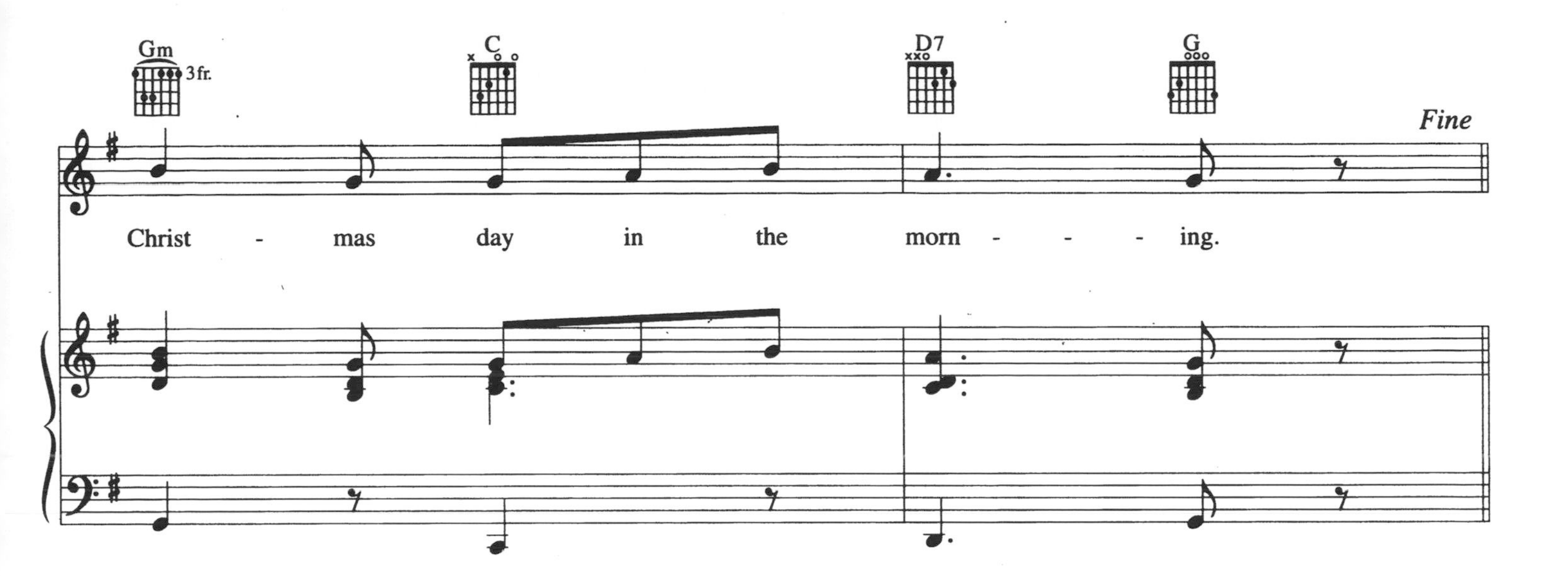

2. And what was in those ships, all three
On Christmas day, on Christmas day?
And what was in those ships, all three
On Christmas day in the morning?

3. The Virgin Mary and Christ were there
On Christmas day, on Christmas day.
The Virgin Mary and Christ were there
On Christmas day in the morning.

Christians Awake

Words by John Byrom
Music by John Wainwright

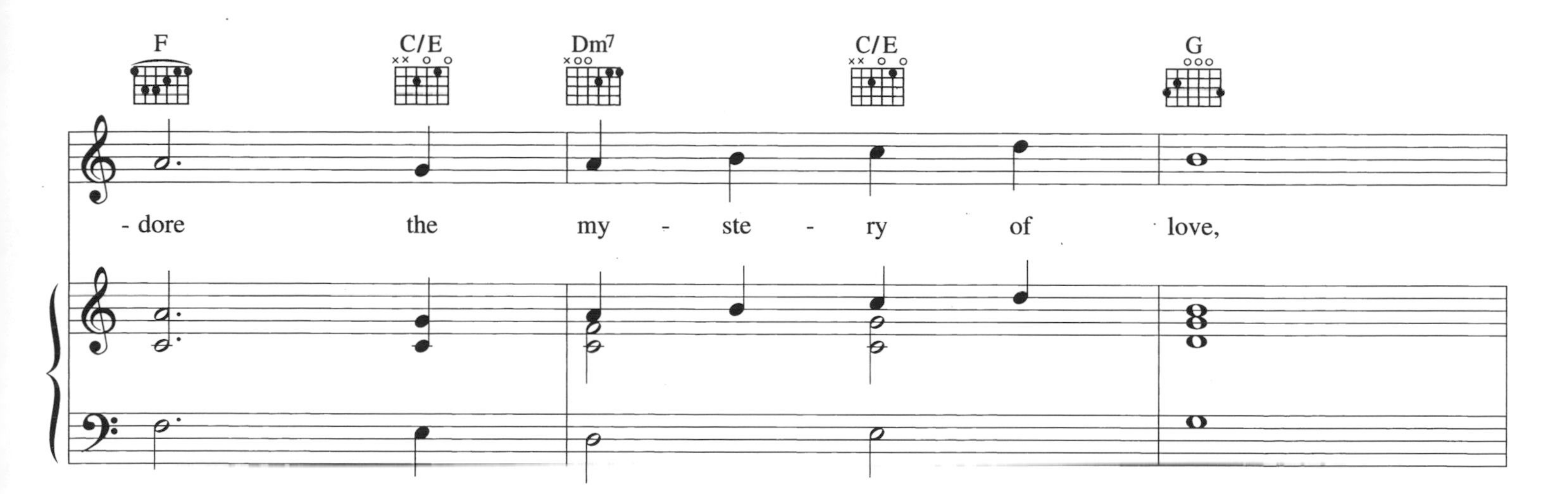
F C/E Dm7 C/E G
-dore the my - ste - ry of love,

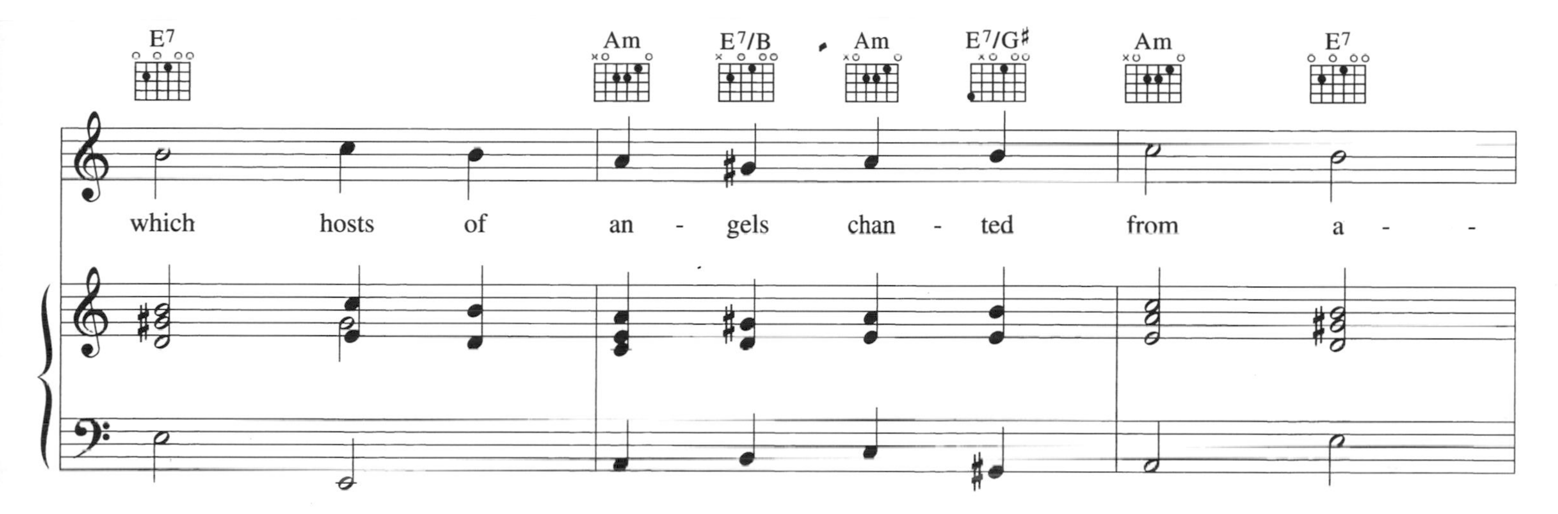
E7 Am E7/B Am E7/G♯ Am E7
which hosts of an - gels chan - ted from a -

Am F G7 C C/E
-bove. With them the joy - - - ful

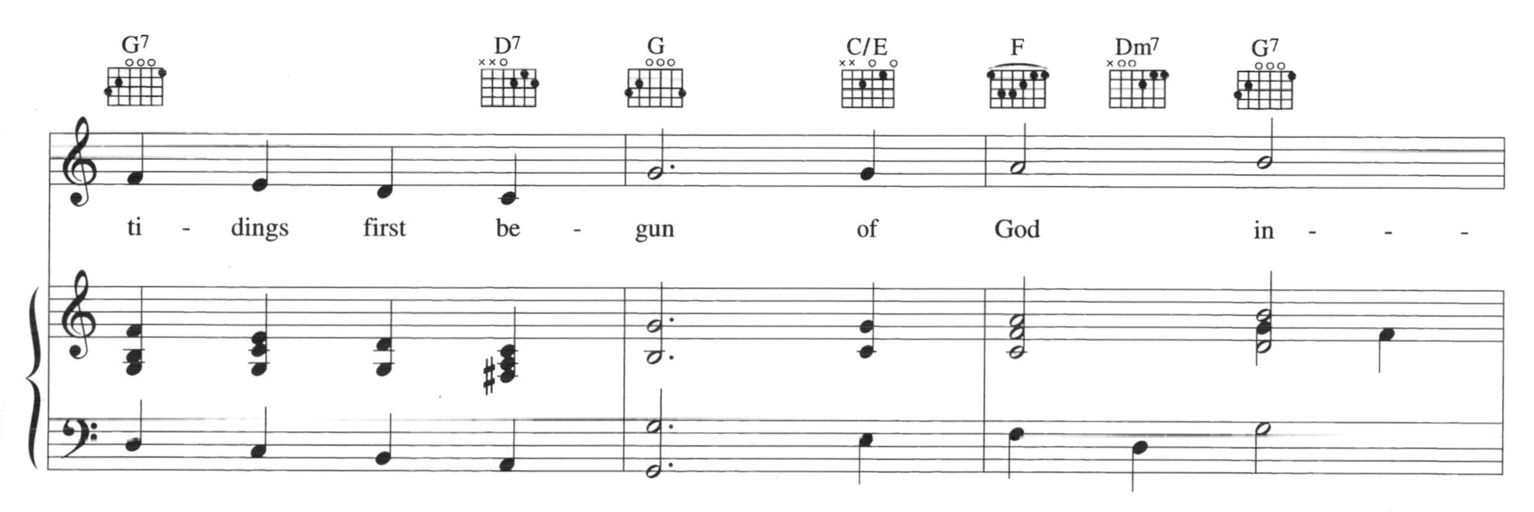
G7 D7 G C/E F Dm7 G7
ti - dings first be - gun of God in - - -

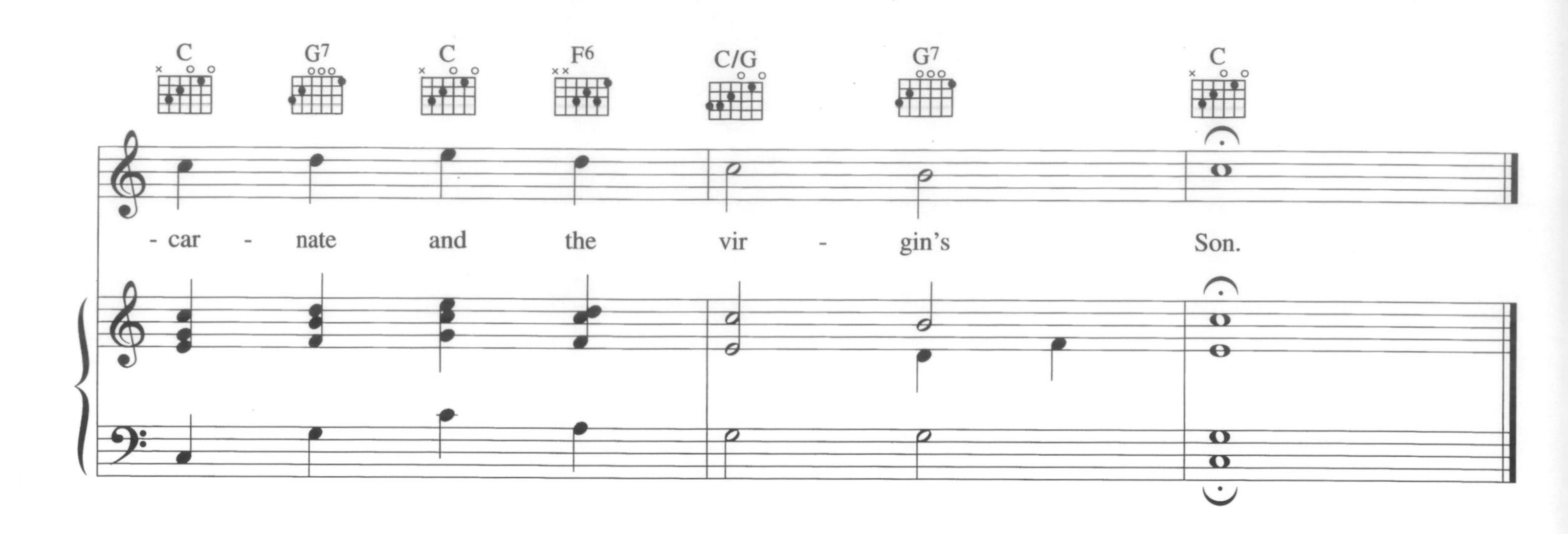

Verse 2:
Then to the watchful shepherds it was told
Who heard th' angelic herald's voice, "Behold
I bring good tidings of a Saviour's birth
To you and all the nations on the earth
This day hath God fulfilled his promised word
This day is born a Saviour, Christ the Lord."

Verse 3:
He spake; and straightway the celestial choir
In hymns of joy, unknown before, conspire;
The praises of redeeming love they sang
And heav'n's whole orb with alleluias rang;
God's highest glory was their anthem still
Peace on the earth, in ev'ry heart good will.

Verse 4:
To Bethl'em straight th'enlightened shepherds ran
To see, unfolding, God's eternal plan
And found, with Joseph and the blessèd maid
Her son, the Saviour, in a manger laid:
Then to their flocks, still praising God, return
And their glad hearts with holy rapture burn.

Verse 5:
O may we keep and ponder in our mind
God's wondrous love in saving lost mankind.
Trace we the babe, who hath retrieved our loss
From his poor manger to his bitter cross
Tread in his steps, assisted by his grace
Till our first heav'nly state again takes place.

Verse 6:
Then may we hope, th'angelic hosts among
To sing, redeemed, a glad triumphal song.
He that was born upon this joyful day
Around us all his glory shall display
Saved by his love, incessant we shall sing
Eternal praise to heav'n's almighty King.

In Dulci Jubilo

Traditional
English Words by R.L. Pearsall

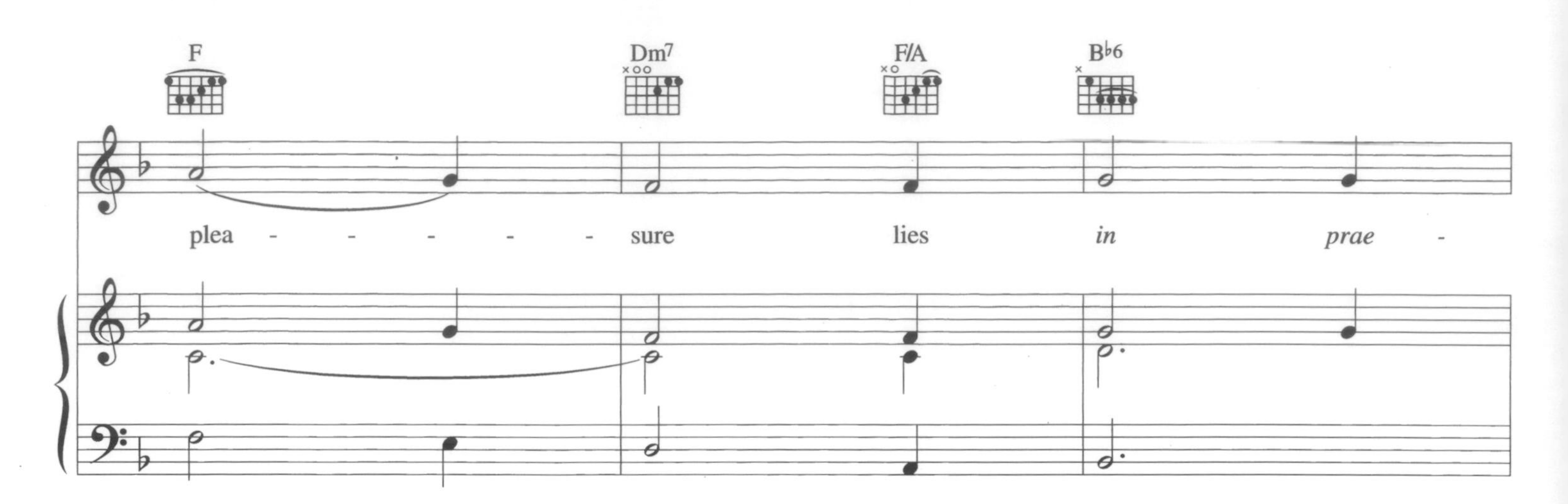
F
Dm7
F/A
B♭6
plea - - - - - sure lies in prae -

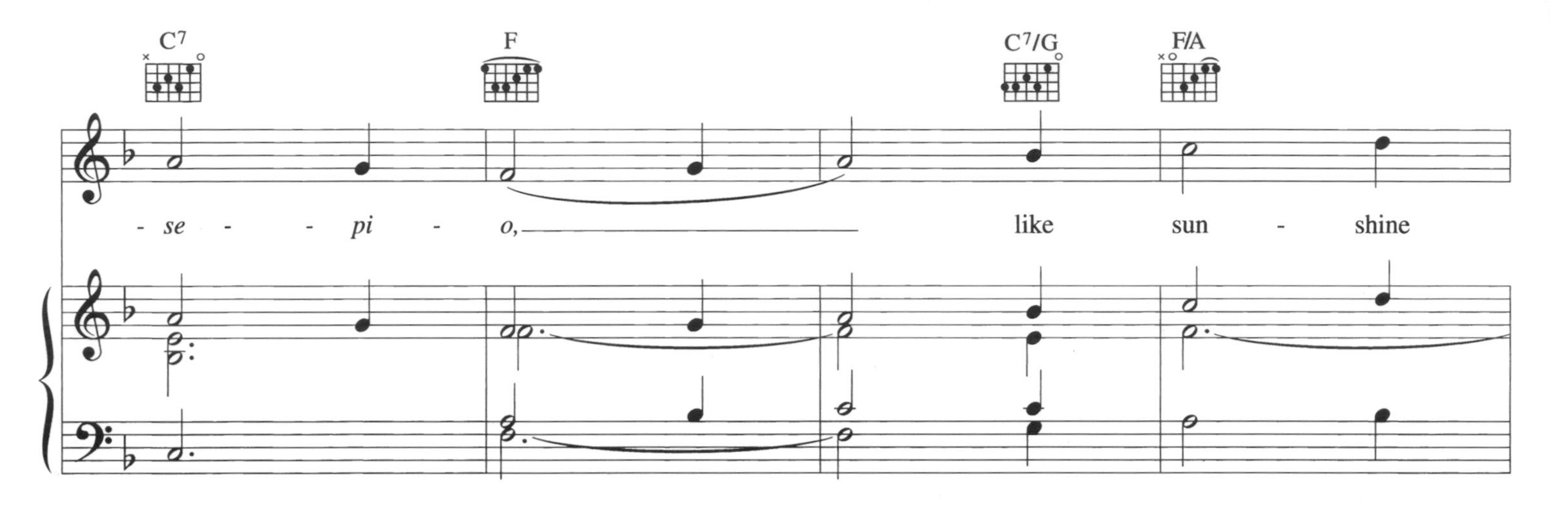
C7
F
C7/G
F/A
- se - - pi - o, like sun - shine

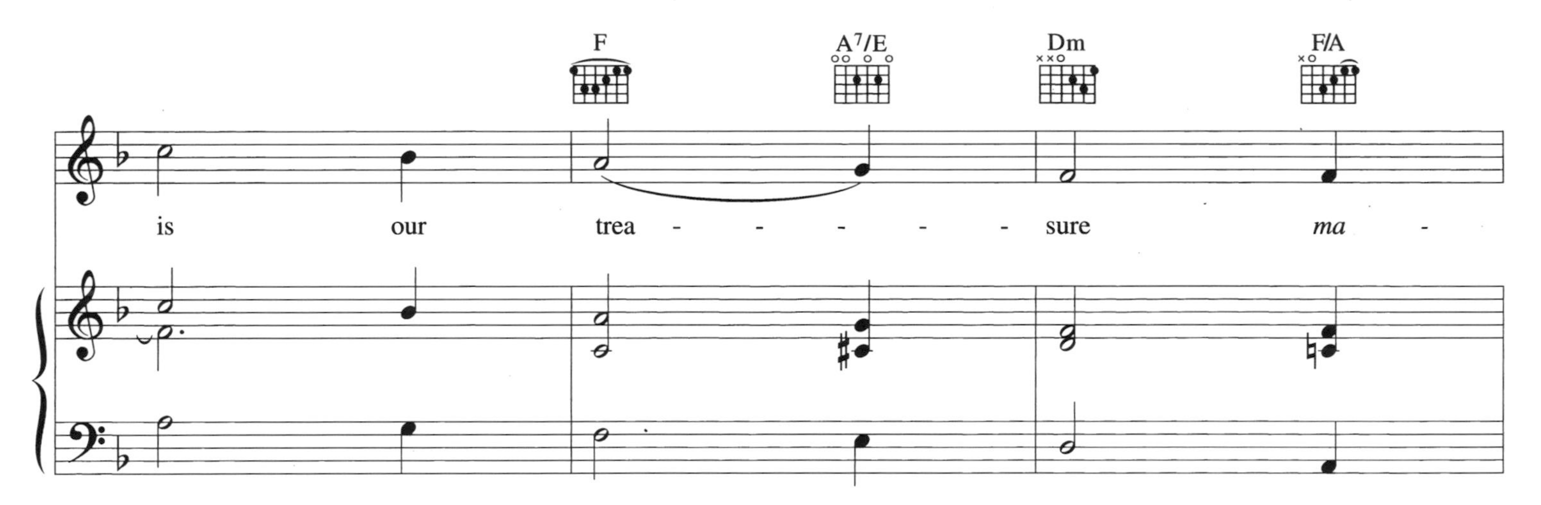
F
A7/E
Dm
F/A
is our trea - - - - - sure ma -

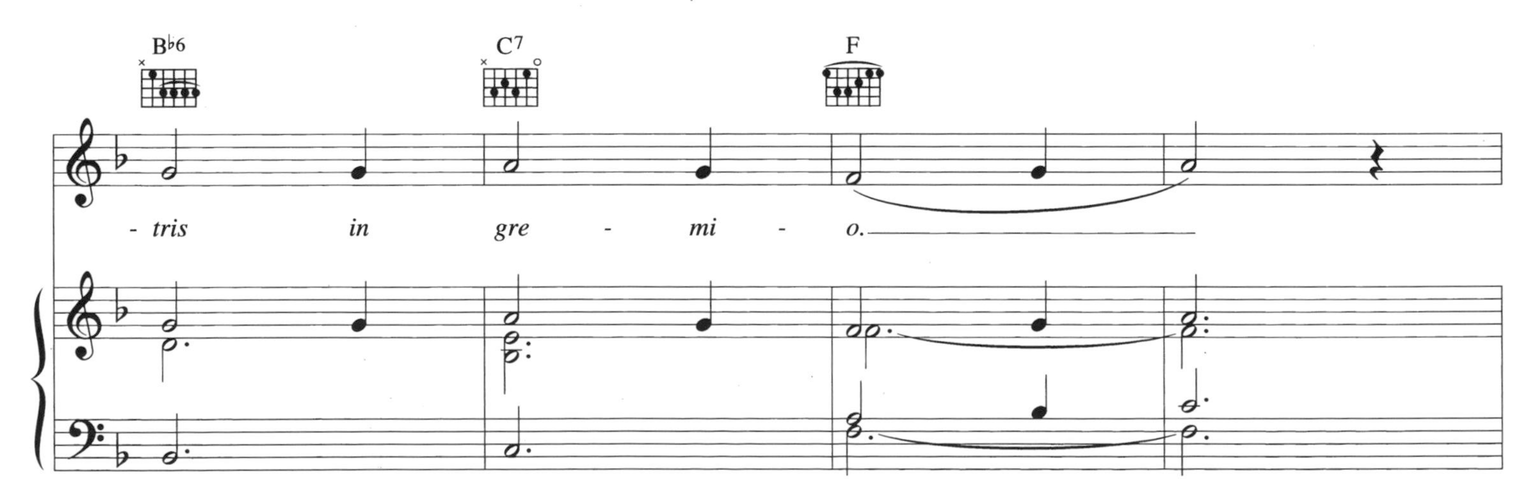
B♭6
C7
F
- tris in gre - mi - o.

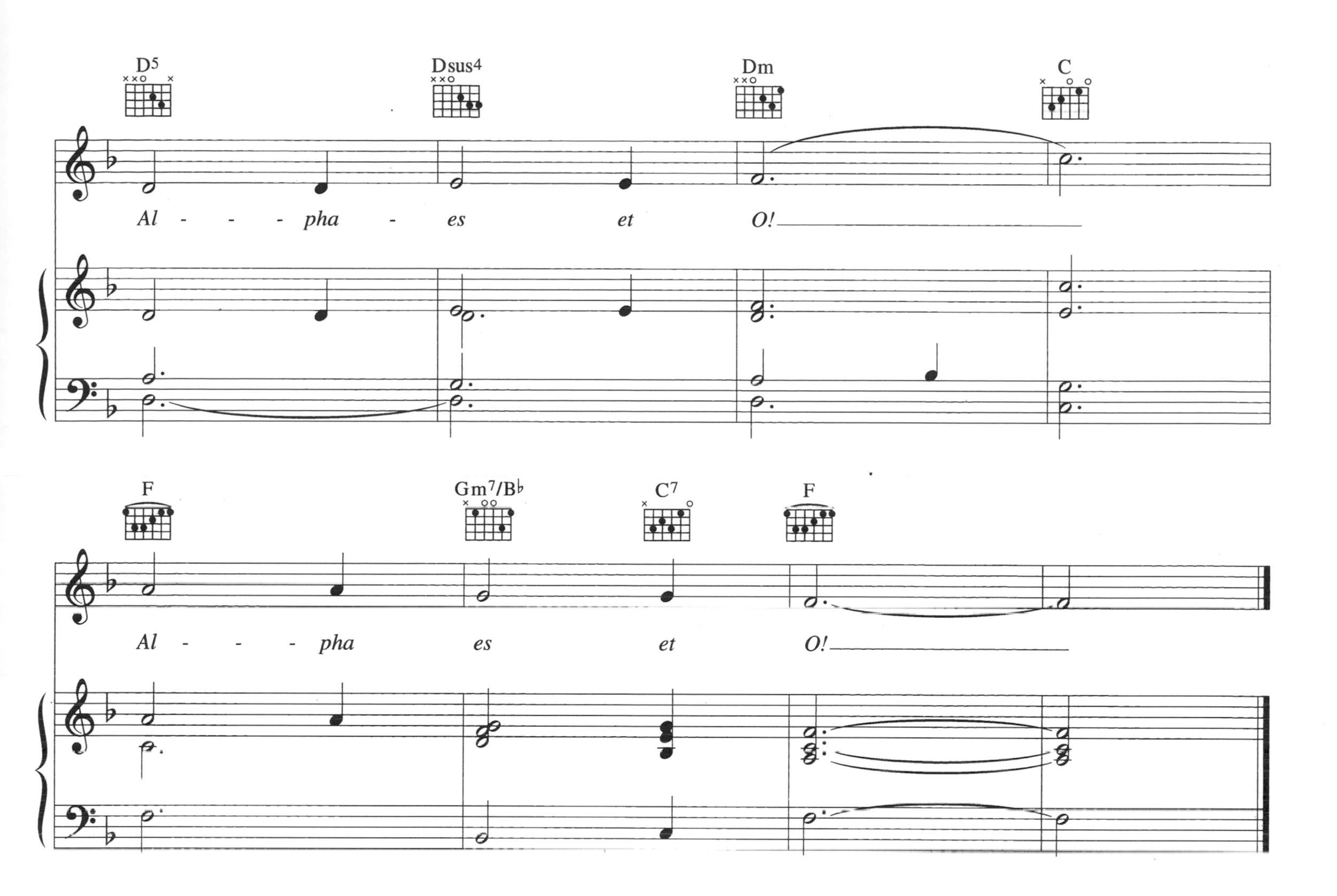

Verse 2:
O Jesu, parvule
For thee I long alway
Comfort my heart's blindness
O puer optime
With all they loving kindness
O princeps gloriae
Trahe me post te! Trahe me post te!

Verse 3:
O Patris caritas!
O Nati lenitas!
Deeply were we stainèd
Per nostra crimina
But thou for us hast gainèd
Coelorum gaudia
O that we were there!

Verse 4:
Ubi sunt gaudia
In any place but there?
There are angels singing
Nova cantica
And there the bells are ringing
In Regis curia
O that we were there!

In The Bleak Midwinter

Words by Christina Rossetti
Music by Gustav Holst

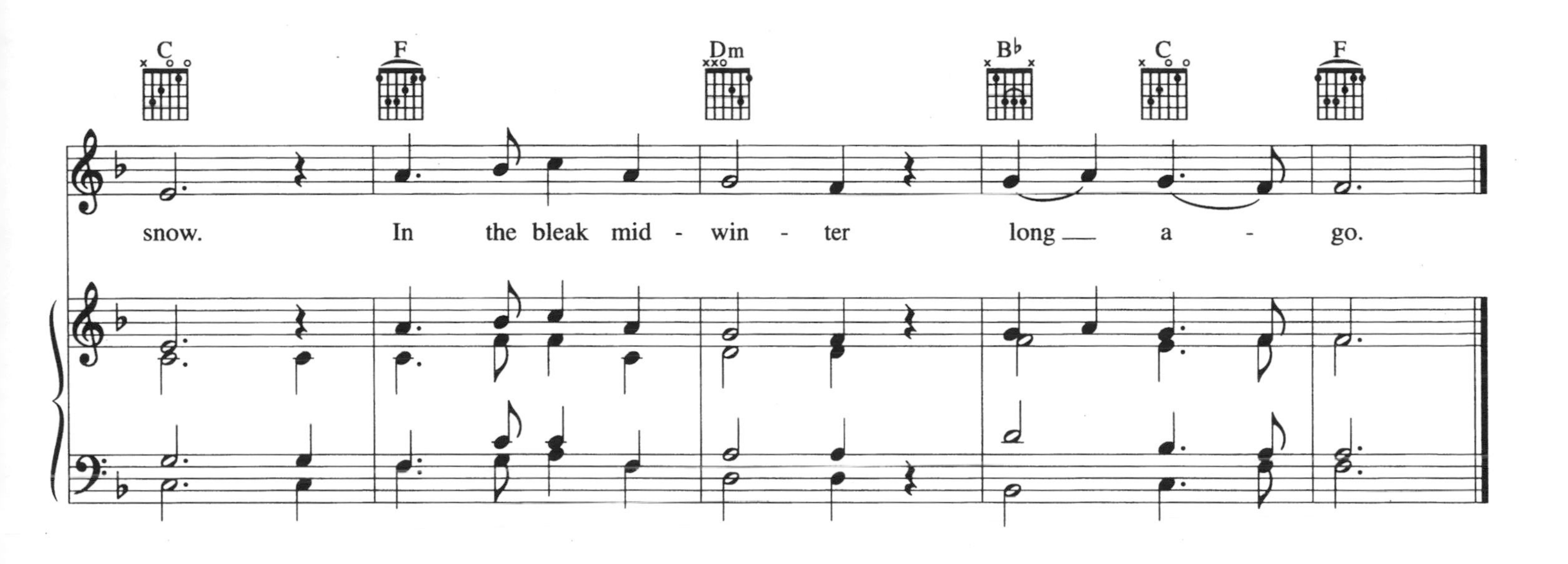

2. Our God, heav'n cannot hold him,
Nor earth sustain
Heav'n and earth shall flee away
When he comes to reign
In the bleak midwinter
A stable-place sufficed
The Lord God Almighty
Jesus Christ.

3. Enough for him whom cherubim
Worship night and day
A breastful of milk
And a manger full of hay
Enough for him, whom angels
Fall down before
The ox and ass and camel
Which adore.

4. Angels and archangels
May have gathered there
Cherubim and seraphim
Thronged the air
But only his mother
In her maiden bliss
Worshipped the Beloved
With a kiss.

5. What can I give him
Poor as I am?
If I were a shepherd
I would bring a lamb
If I were a wise man
I would do my part
Yet what I can I give him
Give my heart.

Infant Holy, Infant Lowly

Traditional Polish Carol
English Words by Edith Reed

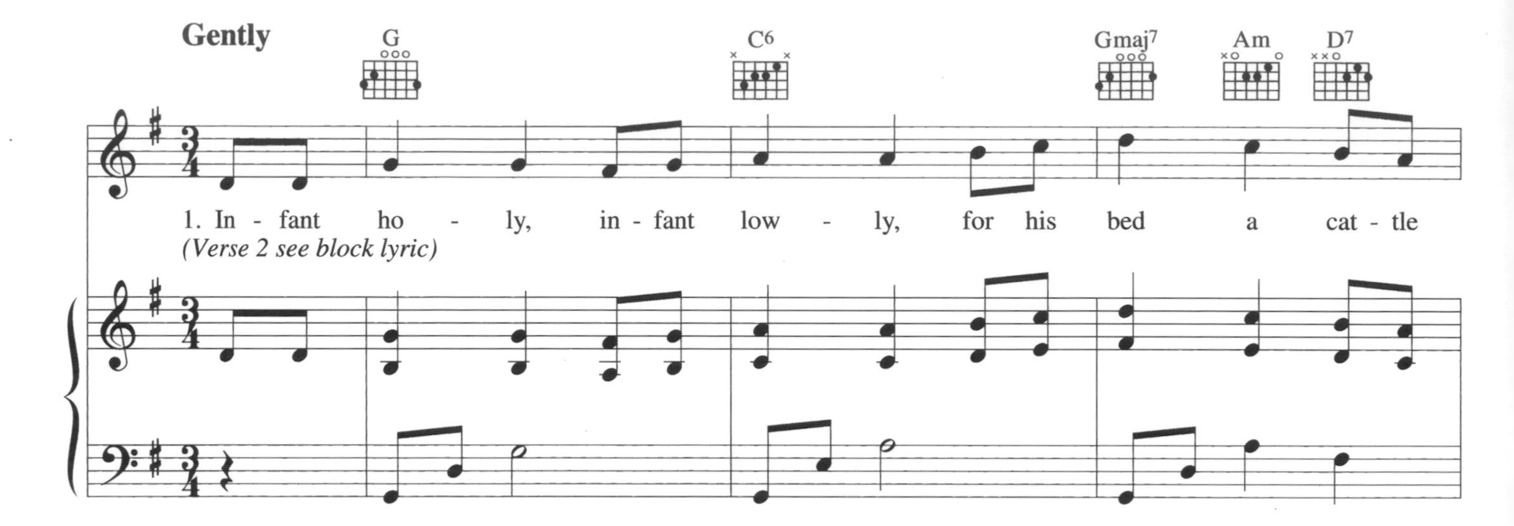

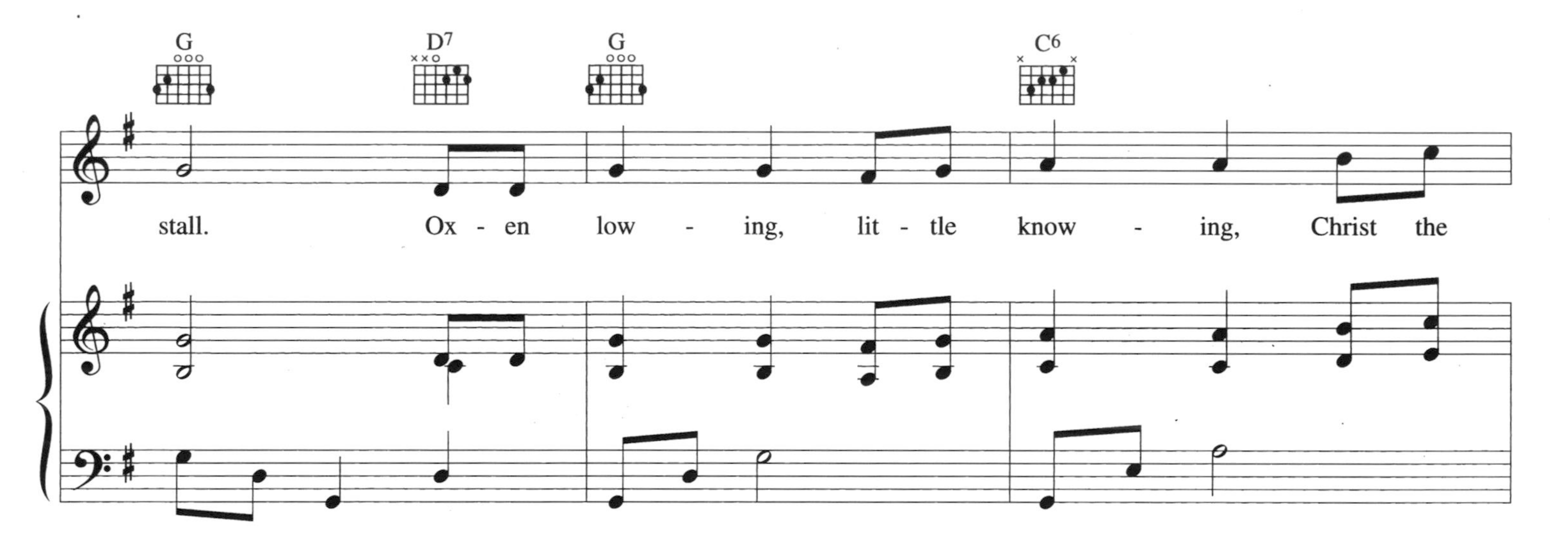

Verse 2:
Flocks were sleeping, shepherds keeping
Vigil till the morning new.
Saw the glory, heard the story
Tidings of a Gospel true
This rejoicing, free from sorrow
Praises voicing, greet the morrow
Christ the babe was born for you
Christ the babe was born for you!

It Came Upon A Midnight Clear

Words by Edmund Hamilton Sears
Music by Richard Storrs Willis

Verse 2:
Still through the cloven skies they come
With peaceful wings unfurled
And still their heav'nly music floats
O'er all the weary world;
Above its sad and lowly plains
They bend on hov'ring wing
And ever o'er its Babel-sounds
The blessèd angels sing.

Verse 3:
Yet with the woes of sin and strife
The world has suffered long.
Beneath the angels' strain have rolled
Two thousand years of wrong,
And man, at war with man hears not
The love-song which they bring
O hush the noise ye men of strife
And hear the angels sing!

Verse 4:
And ye, beneath life's crushing load
Whose forms are bending low
Who toil along the climbing way
With painful steps and slow
Look now! for glad and golden hours
Come swiftly on the wing
O rest beside the weary road
And hear the angels sing.

Verse 5:
For lo! the days are hast'ning on
By prophet bards fore-told
When, with the ever-circling years
Comes round the Age of Gold
When peace shall over all the earth
Its ancient splenders fling
And all the world give back the song
Which now the angels sing.

Joy To The World

Music by George Frideric Handel
Words by Isaac Watts

Verse 2:
Joy to the earth! The Saviour reigns
Let us our songs employ.
While fields and floods, rocks, hills and plains
Repeat the sounding joy
Repeat the sounding joy
Repeat, repeat the sounding joy.

Verse 3:
He rules the world with truth and grace
And makes the nations prove
The glories of his righteousness
And wonders of his love
And wonders of his love
And wonders, and wonders of his love.

Lullay My Liking

Words: Traditional
Music by Gustav Holst

sing; She lul - led a lit - tle child, a swee - te lord - ing.

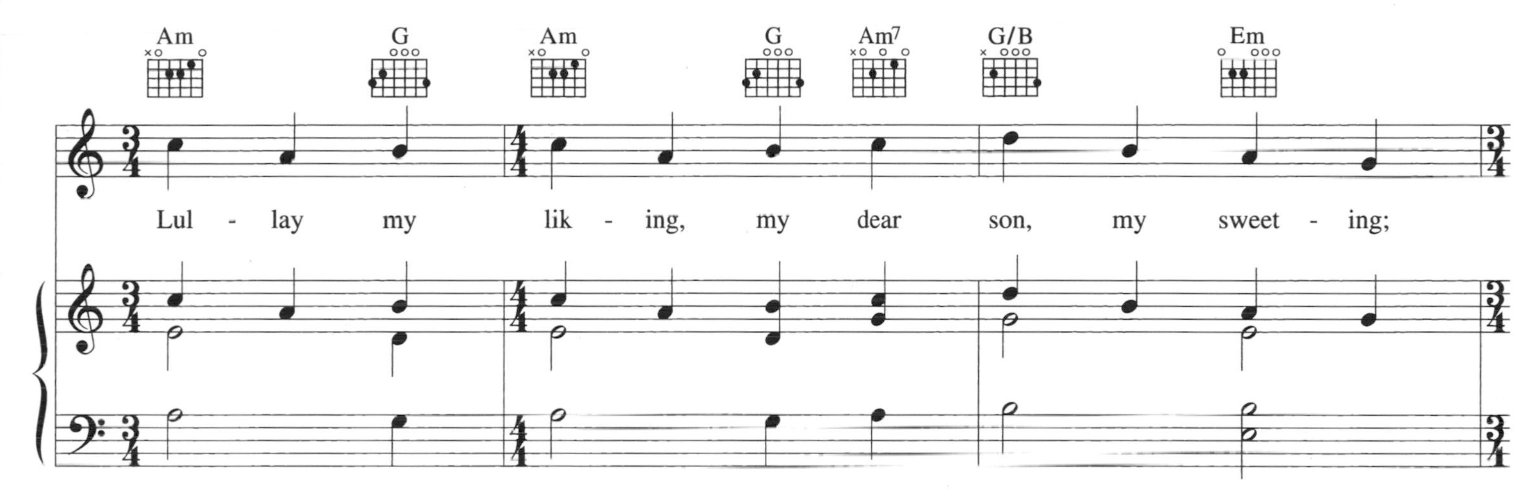
Am G Am G Am7 G/B Em
Lul - lay my lik - ing, my dear son, my sweet - ing;

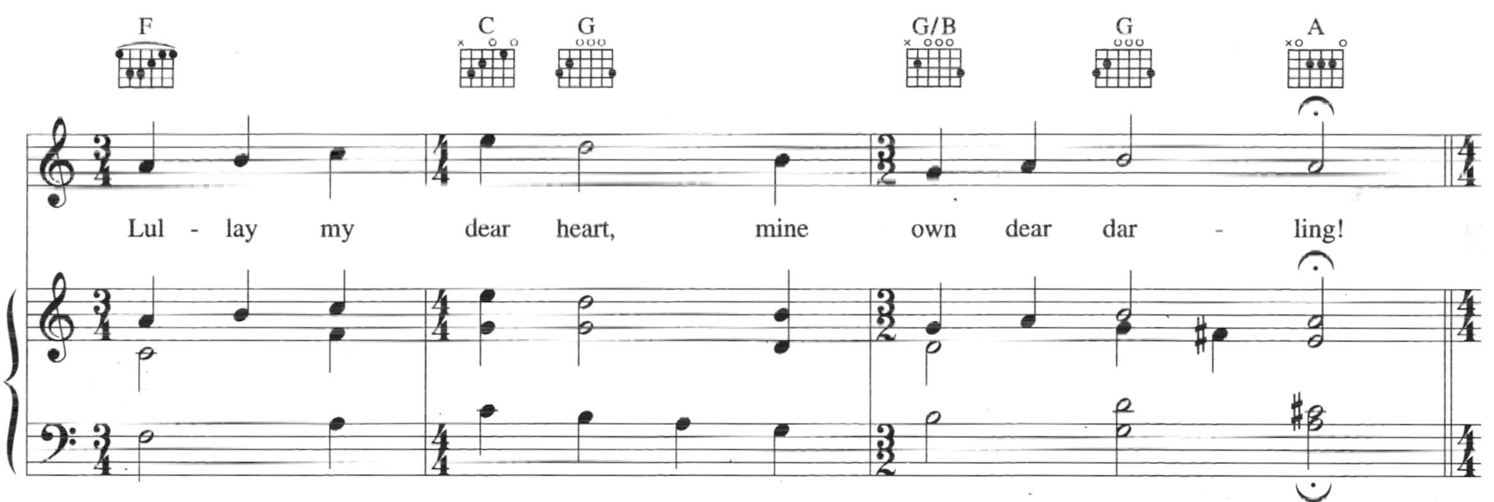
F C G G/B G A
Lul - lay my dear heart, mine own dear dar - ling!

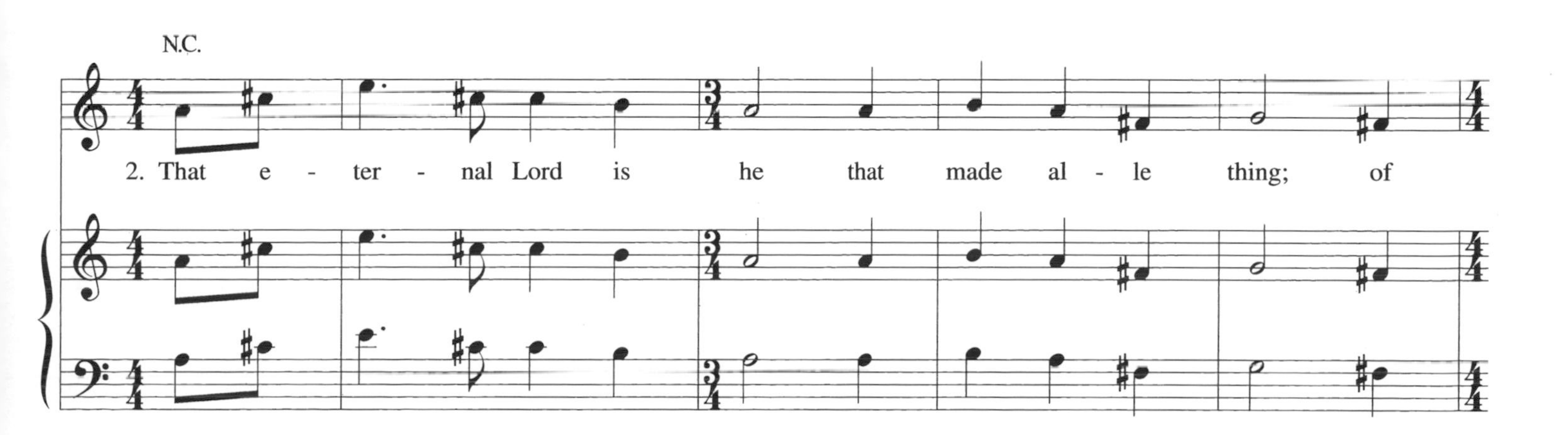
N.C.
2. That e - ter - nal Lord is he that made al - le thing; of

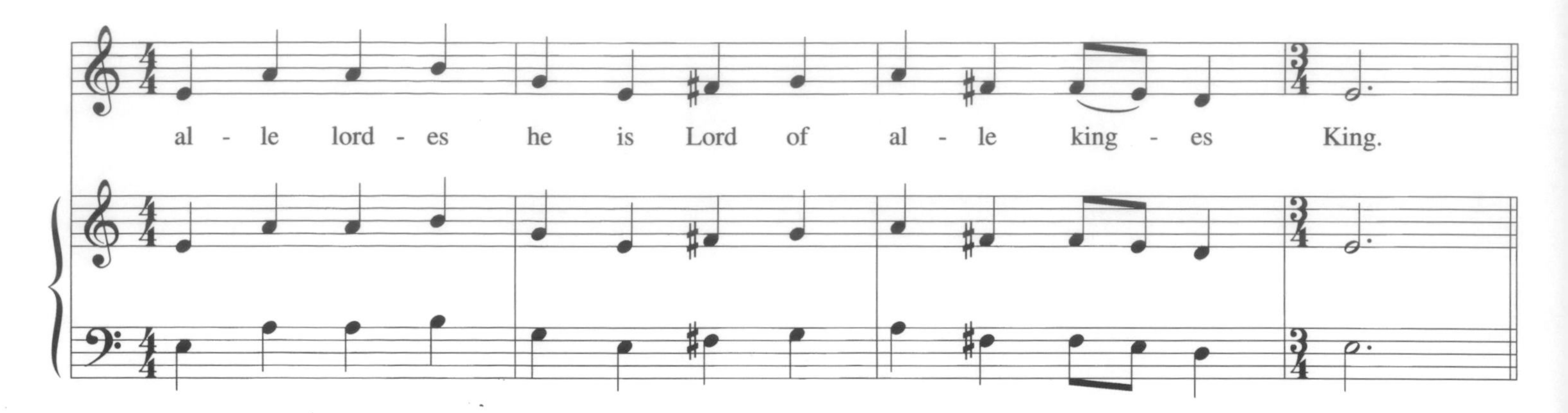
al - le lord - es he is Lord of al - le king - es King.

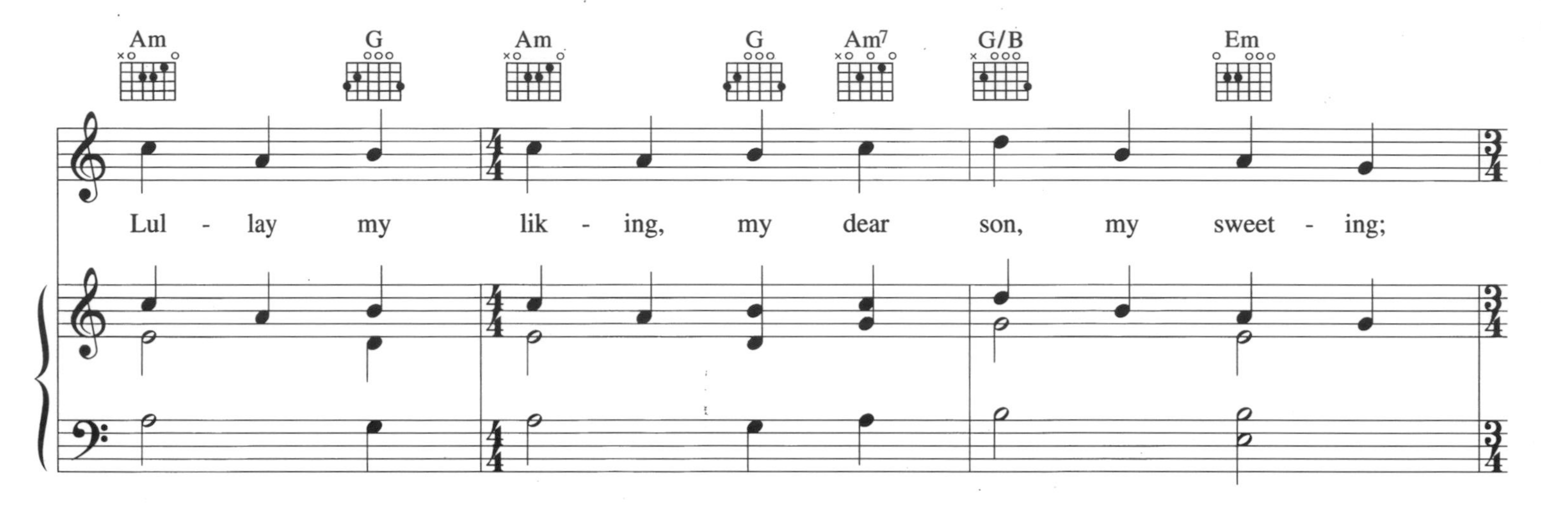
Am G Am G Am7 G/B Em
Lul - lay my lik - ing, my dear son, my sweet - ing;

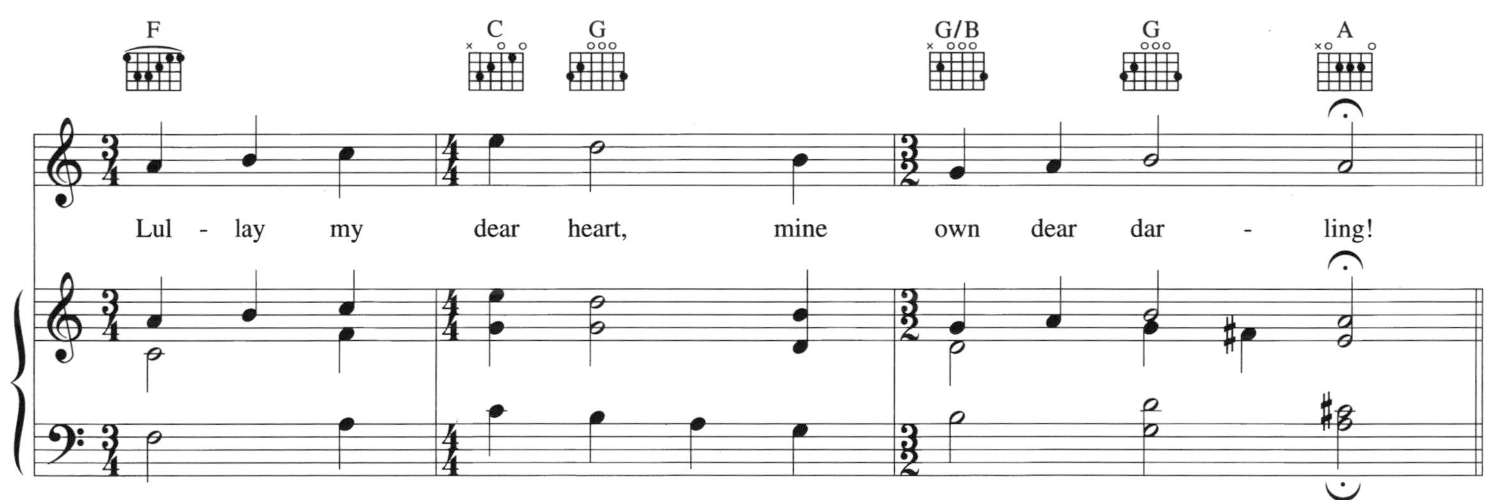
F C G G/B G A
Lul - lay my dear heart, mine own dear dar - ling!

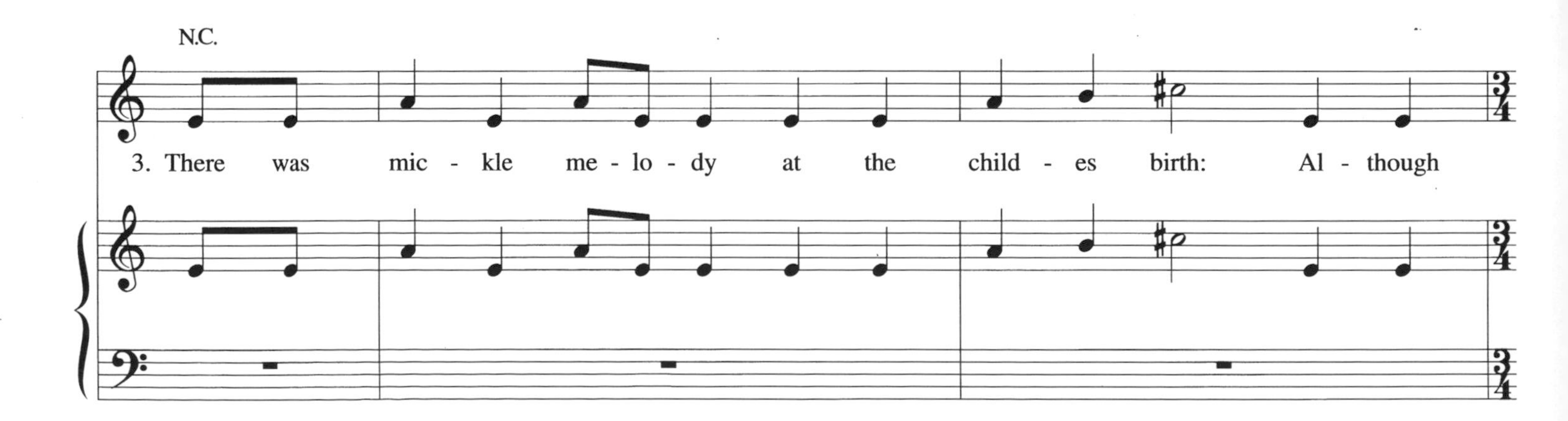
N.C.
3. There was mic - kle me - lo - dy at the child - es birth: Al - though

they were in hea - ven's bliss they ma - de mic - kle mirth.

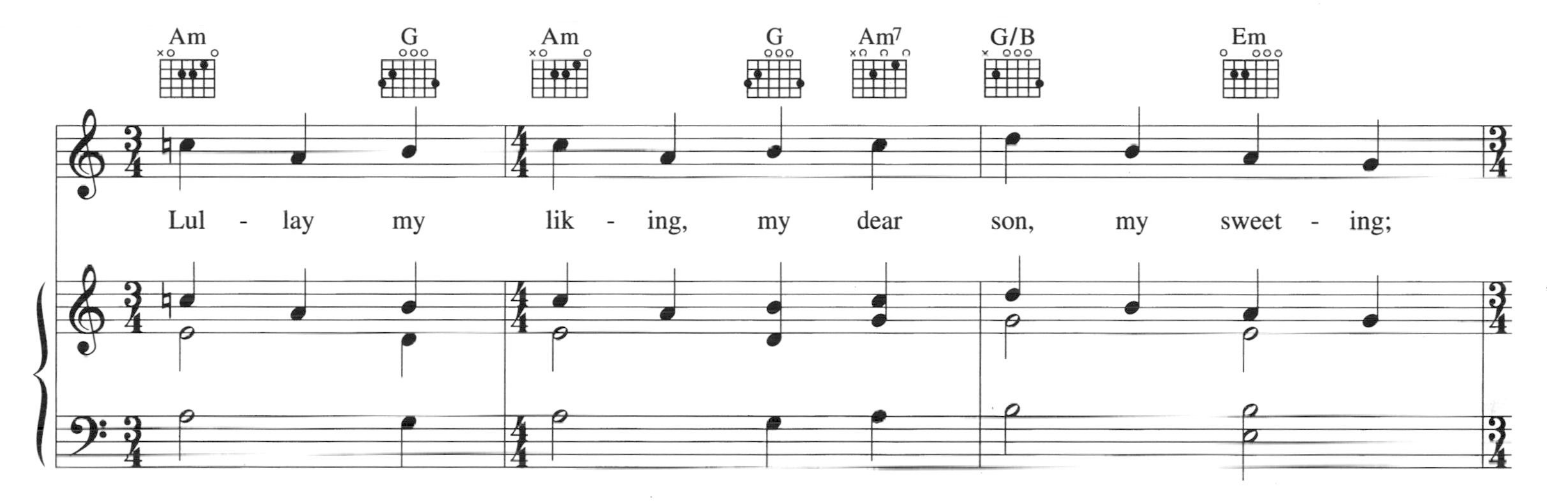
Am G Am G Am7 G/B Em
Lul - lay my lik - ing, my dear son, my sweet - ing;

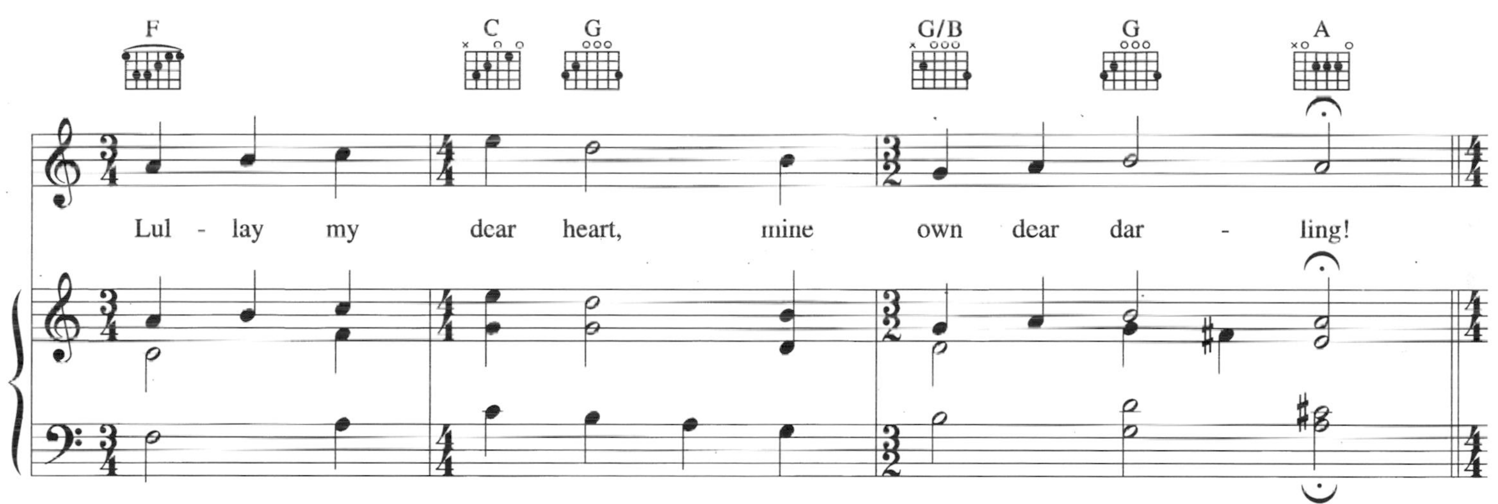
F C G G/B G A
Lul - lay my dear heart, mine own dear dar - ling!

N.C.
4. An - gels bright they sang that night and said - en to that

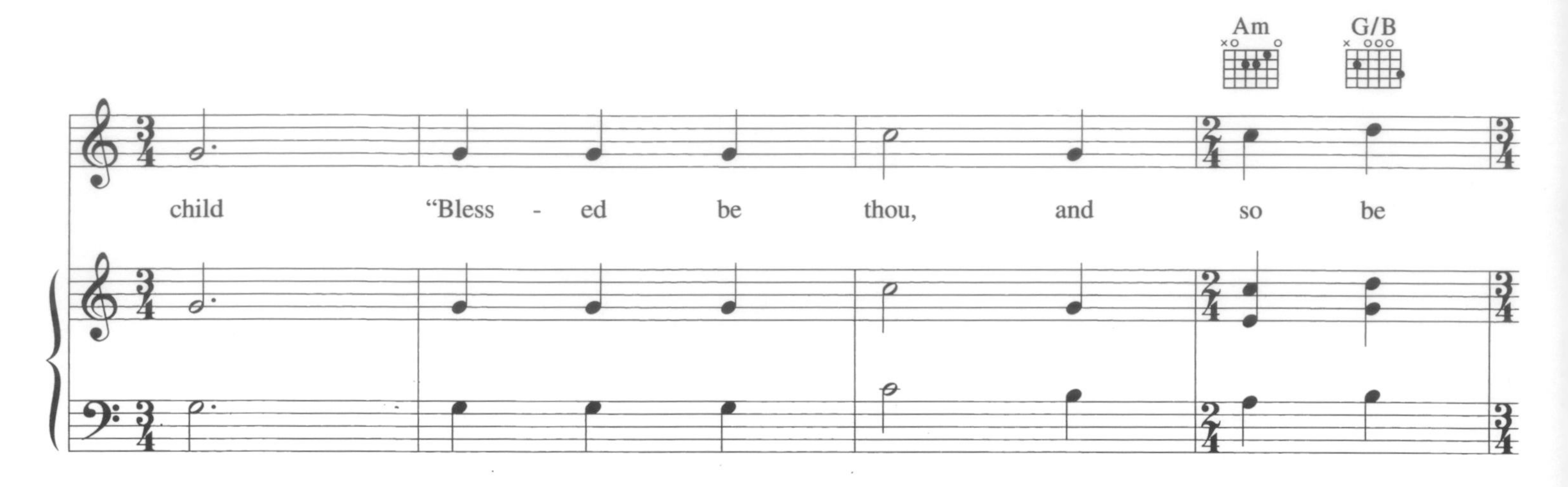
Am
G/B
child "Bless - ed be thou, and so be

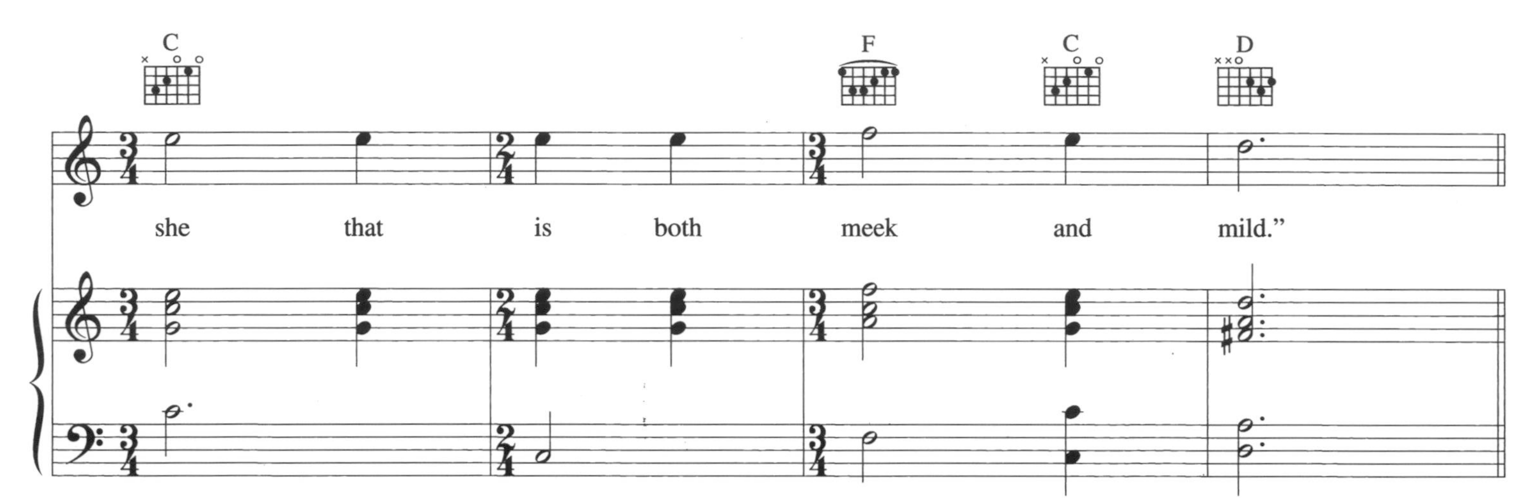
C
F
C
D
she that is both meek and mild."

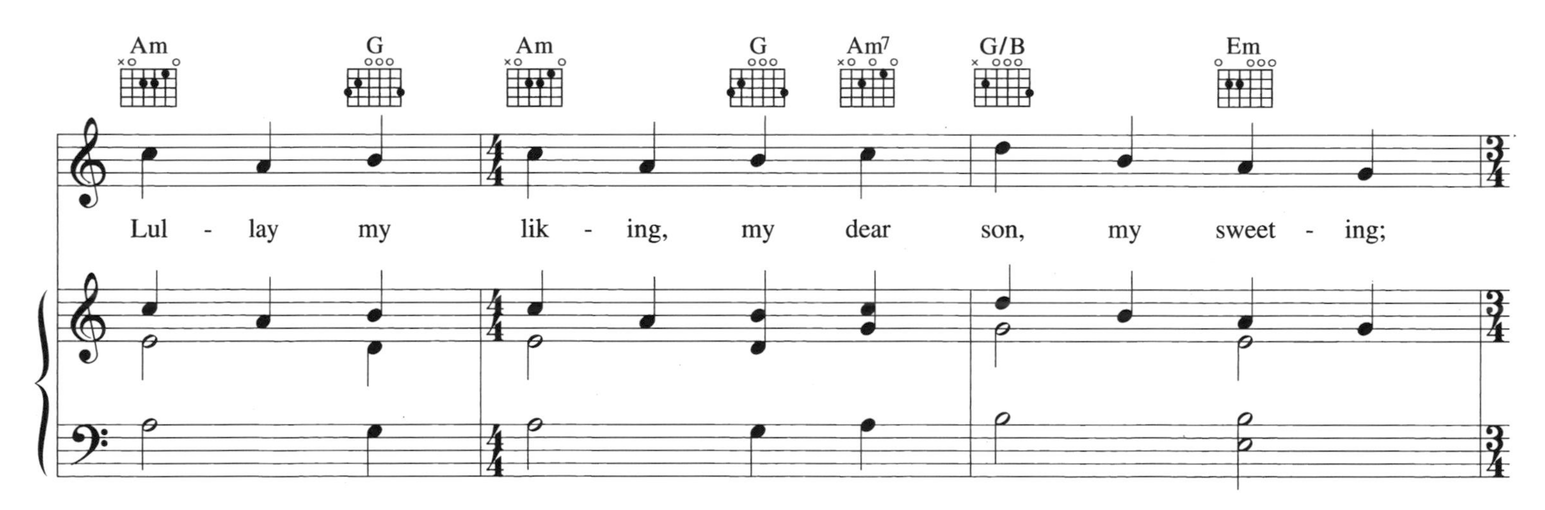
Am
G
Am
G
Am7
G/B
Em
Lul - lay my lik - ing, my dear son, my sweet - ing;

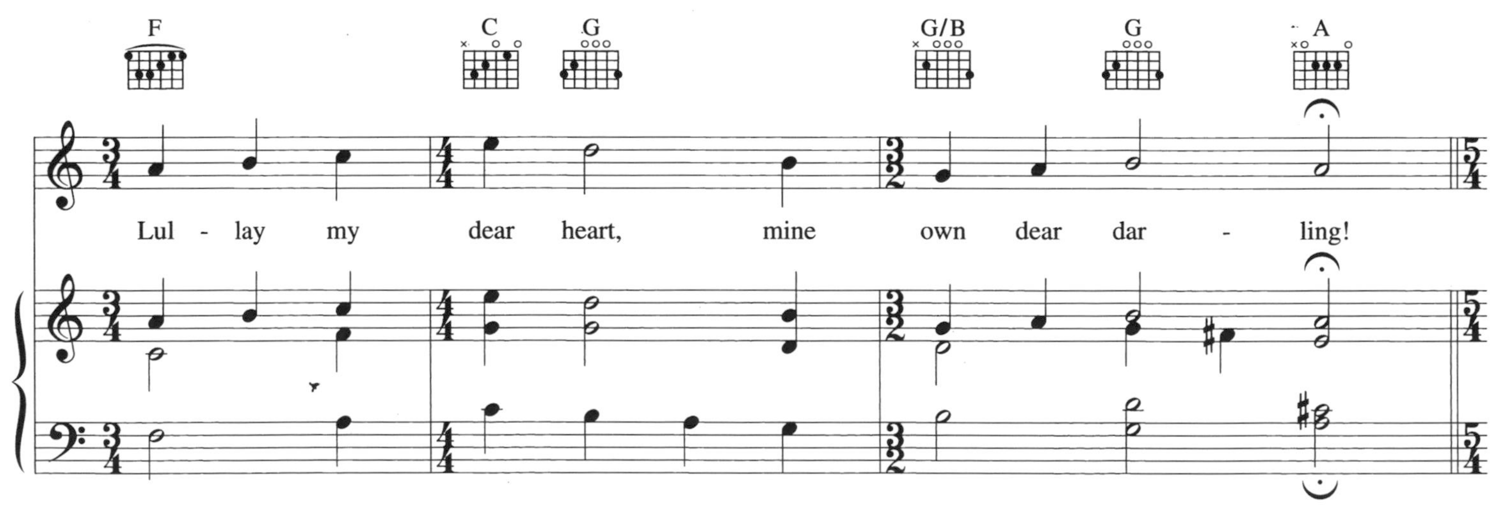
F
C
G
G/B
G
A
Lul - lay my dear heart, mine own dear dar - ling!

N.C.
5. Pray we now to that child, and to his mo - ther dear, God
grant them all his bless - ing that now mak - en cheer.

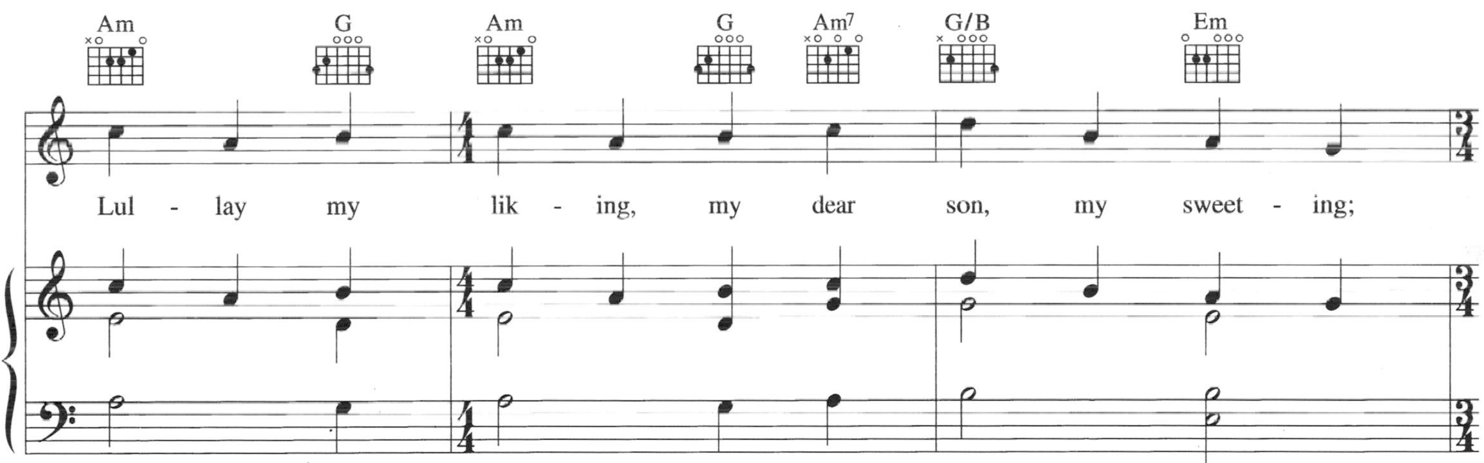
Am G Am G Am7 G/B Em
Lul - lay my lik - ing, my dear son, my sweet - ing;

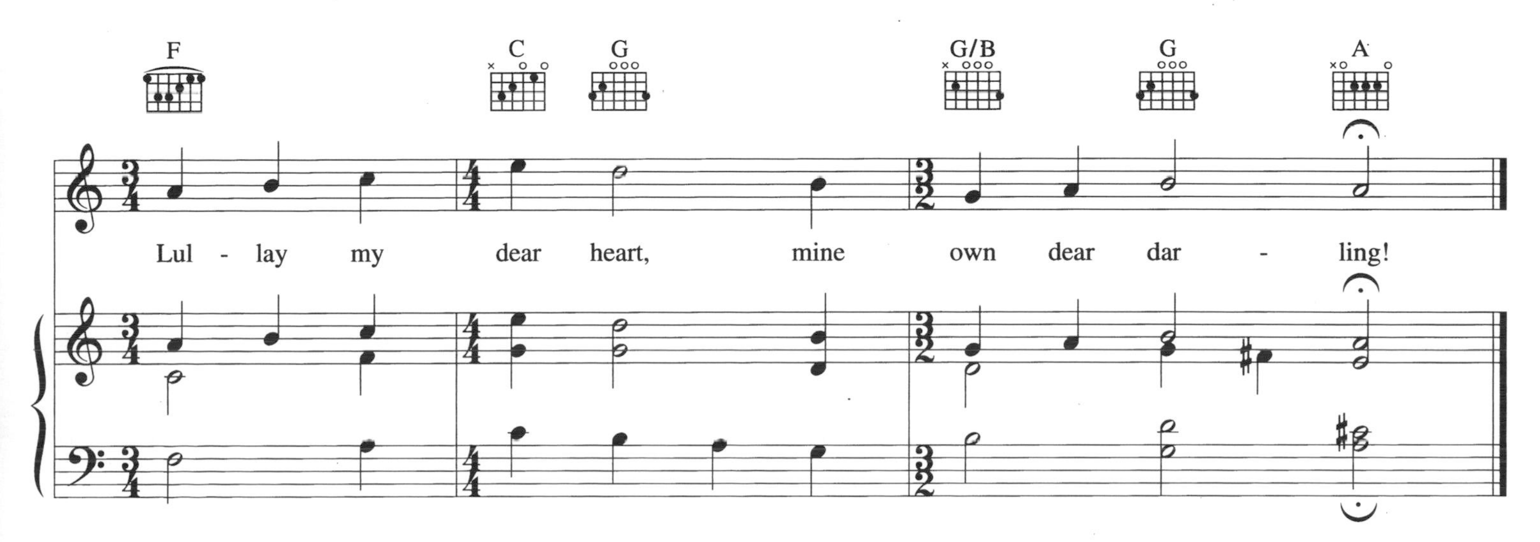
F C G G/B G A
Lul - lay my dear heart, mine own dear dar - ling!

Mary Had A Baby

Traditional Afro-American Spiritual

Verse 2:
What did she name him, oh Lord?
What did she name him, oh my Lord?
What did she name him, oh Lord?
The people keep a-comin' and the train done gone.

Verse 3:
She called him Jesus, oh Lord
She called him Jesus, oh my Lord
She called him Jesus, oh Lord
The people keep a-comin' and the train done gone.

Verse 4:
Now where was he born, oh Lord?
Where was he born, oh my Lord?
Where was he born, oh Lord?
The people keep a-comin' and the train done gone.

Verse 5:
Born in a stable, oh Lord
Born in a stable, oh my Lord
Born in a stable, oh Lord
The people keep a-comin' and the train done gone.

Verse 6:
Where did they lay him, oh Lord?
Where did they lay him, oh my Lord?
Where did they lay him, oh Lord?
The people keep a-comin' and the train done gone.

Verse 7:
Laid him a in manger, oh Lord
Laid him a in manger, oh my Lord
Laid him a in manger, oh Lord
The people keep a-comin' and the train done gone.

Verse 8:
Who came to see him, oh Lord?
Who came to see him, oh my Lord?
Who came to see him, oh Lord?
The people keep a-comin' and the train done gone.

Verse 9:
Shepherds came to see him, oh Lord
Shepherds came to see him, oh my Lord
Shepherds came to see him, oh Lord
The people keep a-comin' and the train done gone.

Verse 10:
The wise men kneeled before him, oh Lord
The wise men kneeled before him, oh my Lord
The wise men kneeled before him, oh Lord
The people keep a-comin' and the train done gone.

Verse 11:
King Herod tried to find him, oh Lord
King Herod tried to find him, oh my Lord
King Herod tried to find him, oh Lord
The people keep a-comin' and the train done gone.

Verse 12:
They went to Egypt, oh Lord
They went to Egypt, oh my Lord
They went to Egypt, oh Lord
The people keep a-comin' and the train done gone.

Verse 13:
Angels watching over him, oh Lord
Angels watching over him, oh my Lord
Angels watching over him, oh Lord
The people keep a-comin' and the train done gone.

My Dancing Day

Traditional

Gracefully

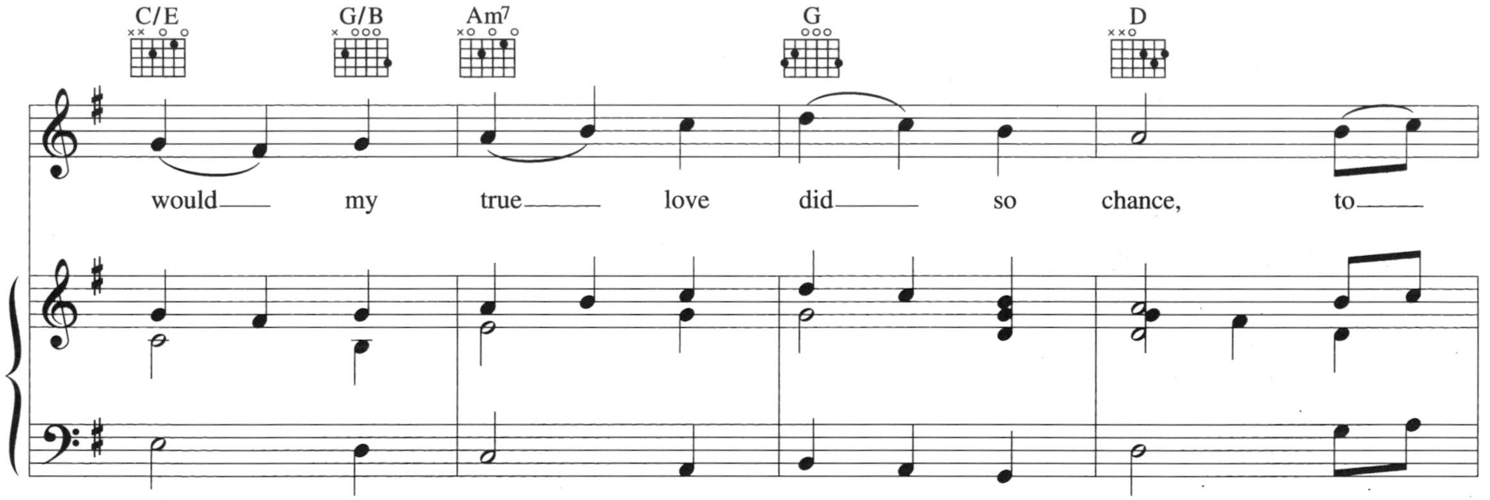

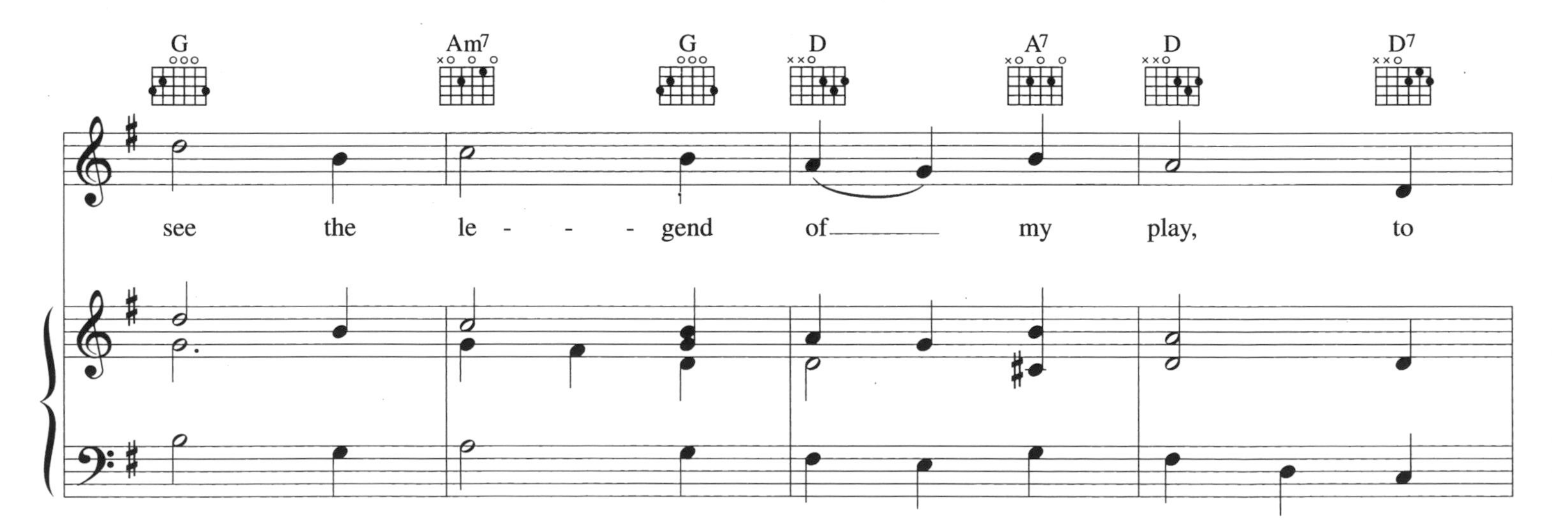

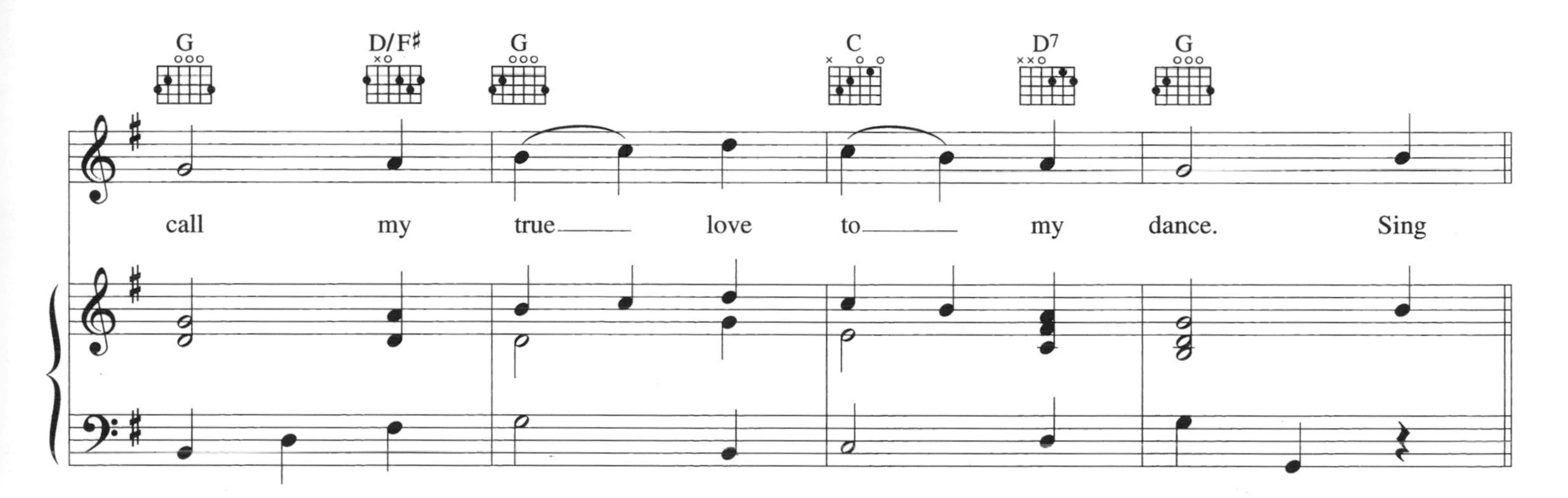

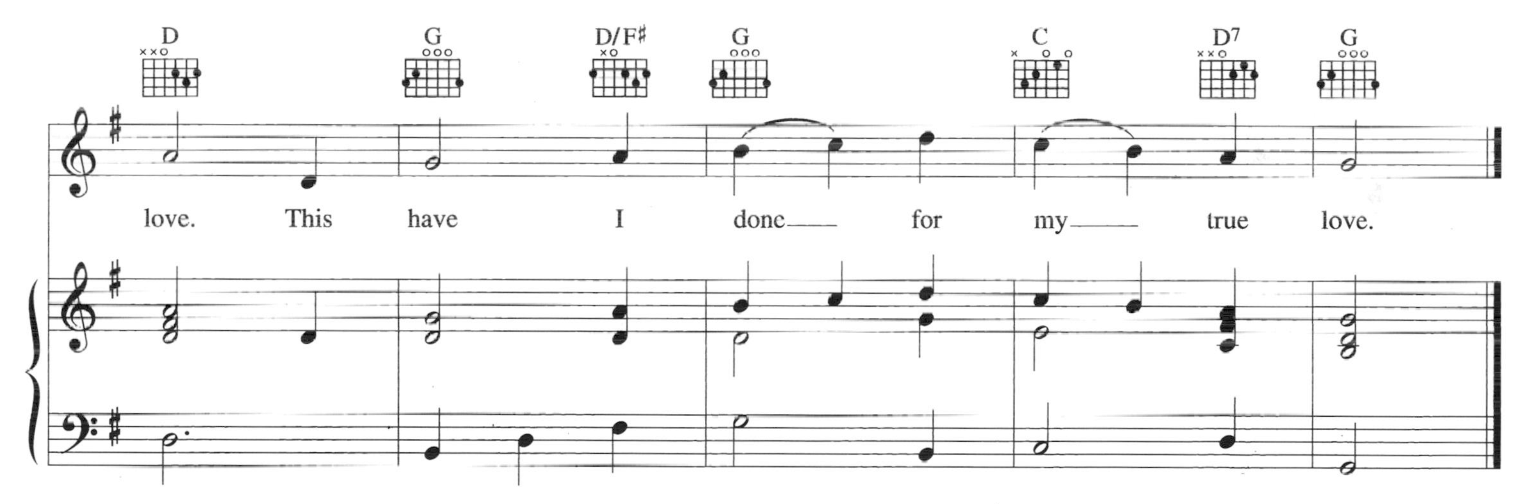

Verse 2:
Then was I born of a virgin pure
Of her I took fleshy substance
Thus was I knit to man's nature
To call true love to my dance.

Sing O my love *etc.*

Verse 3:
In a manger laid and wrapped I was
So very poor, this was my chance
Betwixt an ox and a silly poor ass
To call my true love to my dance.

Sing O my love *etc.*

Verse 4:
Then afterwards baptized I was
The Holy Ghost on me did glance
My Father's voice heard from above
To call my true love to my dance.

Sing O my love *etc.*

O Christmas Tree

(O Tannenbaum)

Traditional

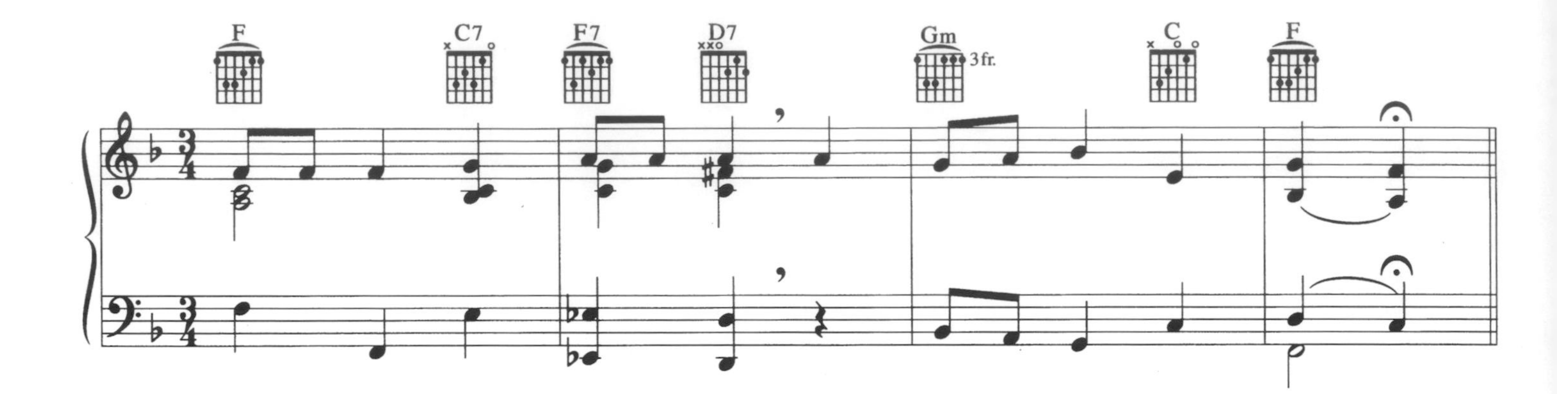

Cm6
D7
F7
Gm 3fr.
D7
Gm 3fr.
C7
Christ - mas tree, you bring us all our
F
C7
wish - es. In ev - 'ry land, in ev - 'ry way, You
F
C
F
A7
bring us hope of peace some - day. O Christ - mas tree, O
Cm6
D7
F7
Gm 3fr.
D7
Gm 3fr.
C7
F
Christ - mas tree, you're tell - ing us it's Christ - mas.

O Come All Ye Faithful

Original Words & Music by John Francis Wade
English Words by Frederick Oakeley

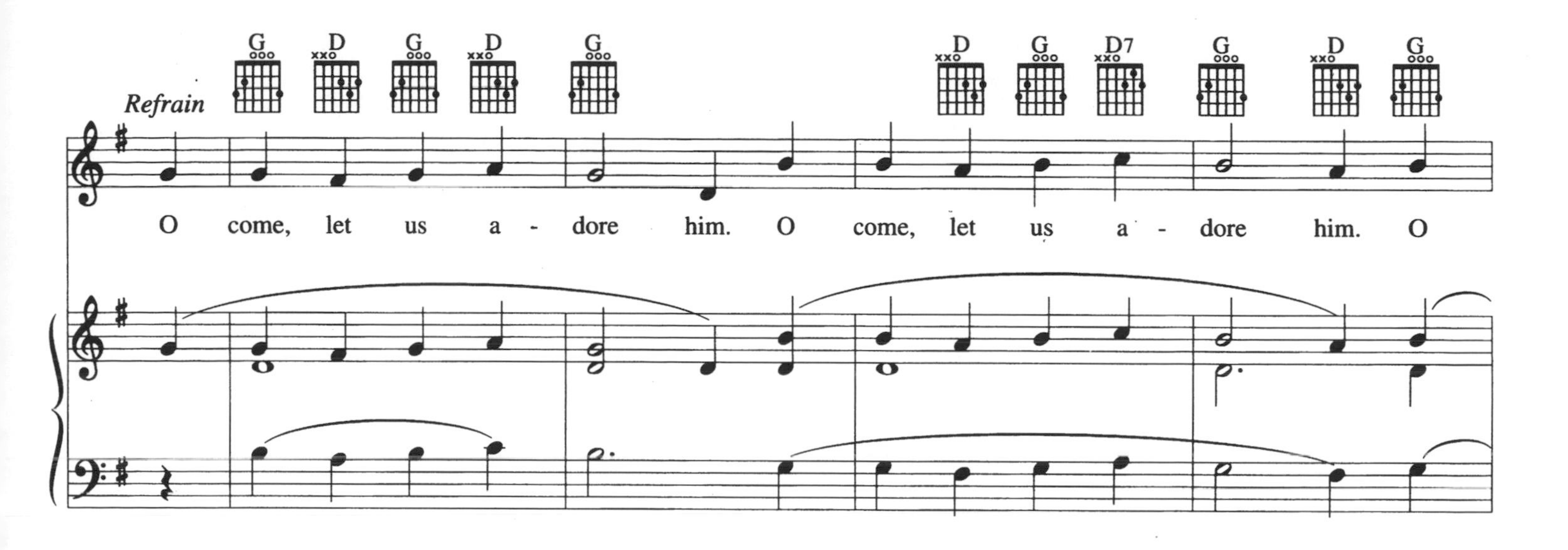

2. Sing, choirs of angels, sing in exultation
O sing all ye citizens of heaven above!
Glory to God, all Glory in the highest.
Refrain

3. Yea, Lord, we greet Thee, born this happy morning
Jesus, to Thee be all glory giv'n;
Word of the Father, now in the flesh appearing.
Refrain

O Come, O Come, Emmanuel

Traditional
English Words by John Neale

Verse 2:
O come, thou rod of Jesse, free
Thine own from Satan's tyranny
From depths of hell thy people save
And give them vict'ry o'er the grave.

Rejoice, rejoice! *etc.*

Verse 3:
O come, thou dayspring, come and cheer
Our spirits by thine advent here
Disperse the gloomy clouds of night
And death's dark shadows put to flight.

Rejoice, rejoice! *etc.*

Verse 4:
O come, thou key of David, come
And open wide our heav'nly home
Make safe the way that leads on high
And close the path to misery.

Rejoice, rejoice! *etc.*

Verse 5:
O come, o come, thou Lord of might
Who to thy tribes on Sinai's height
In ancient times didst give the Law
In cloud and majesty and awe.

Rejoice, rejoice! *etc.*

O Little Town Of Bethlehem

Words by Phillips Brooks
Music by Lewis Redner

2. O morning stars, together
Proclaim the holy birth
And praises sing to God the King
And peace to men on earth
For Christ is born of Mary
And gathered all above.
While mortals sleep
The angels keep
Their watch of wond'ring love

3. How silently, how silently
The wondrous gift is given!
So God imparts to human hearts
The blessing of his heaven
No ear may hear His coming
But in this world of sin
Where meek souls will receive Him still
The dear Christ enters in.

4. Where children pure and happy
Pray to the blessèd child
Where misery cries out to thee
Son of the mother mild
Where charity stands watching
And faith holds wide the door
The dark night wakes, the glory breaks
And Christmas comes once more.

5. O holy child of Bethlehem!
Descend to us, we pray
Cast out our sin, and enter in
Be born in us today
We hear the Christmas angels
The great glad tidings tell
O come to us abide with us
Our Lord Emmanuel.

Once In Royal David's City

Words by Cecil Alexander
Music by Henry Gauntlett

2. He came down to earth from Heaven
Who is God and Lord of all
And His shelter was a stable
And His cradle was a stall
With the poor, and mean, and lowly
Lived on earth our Saviour Holy.

3. And, through all His wondrous Childhood
He would honour and obey
Love and watch the lowly Maiden
In whose gentle arms He lay
Christian children all must be
Mild, obedient, good as He.

4. For He is our childhood's pattern
Day by day like us He grew
He was little, weak and helpless
Tears and smiles like us He knew
And He feeleth for our sadness
And He shareth in our gladness.

5. And our eyes at last shall see Him
Through His own redeeming love
For that Child so dear and gentle
Is our Lord in heaven above
And He leads His children on
To the place where He is gone.

6. Not in that poor lowly stable
With the oxen standing by
We shall see Him, but in Heaven
Sat at God's right hand on high
When like stars His children crown'd
All in white shall wait around.

Past Three O'Clock

Words: Traditional
Music by George Woodward

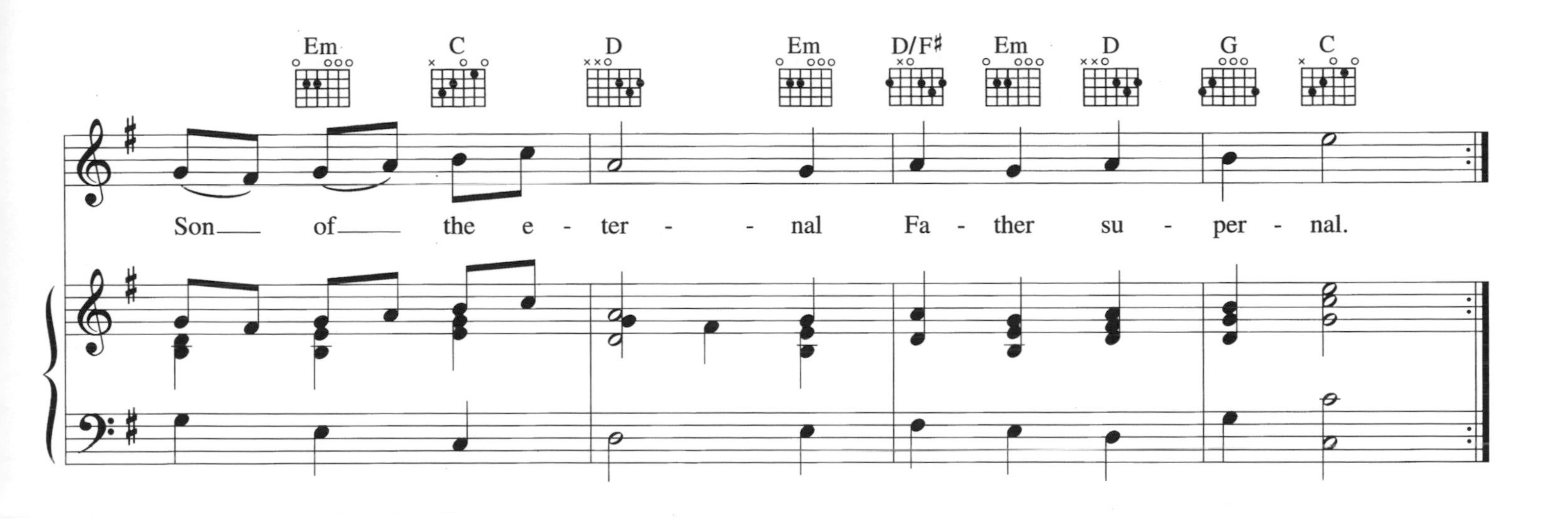

Verse 2:
Seraph quire singeth
Angel bell ringeth
Hark how they rime it
Time it, and chime it.

Past three o'clock *etc.*

Verse 3:
Mid earth rejoices
Hearing such voices
Ne'ertofore so well
Carolling, Nowell.

Past three o'clock *etc.*

Verse 4:
Hinds o'er the pearly
Dewy lawn early
Seek the high stranger
Laid in the manger.

Past three o'clock *etc.*

Verse 5:
Cheese from the dairy
Bring they for Mary
And, not for money
Butter and honey.

Past three o'clock *etc.*

Verse 6:
Light out of star-land
Leadeth from far land
Princes, to meet him
Worship and greet him.

Past three o'clock *etc.*

Verse 7:
Myrrh from full coffer
Incense they offer
Nor is the golden
Nugget witholden.

Past three o'clock *etc.*

Verse 8:
Thus they: I pray you
Up, sirs, nor stay you
Till ye confess him
Likewise, and bless him.

Past three o'clock *etc.*

Quem Pastores
(Shepherds Left Their Flocks A-Straying)

Music: Traditional
English Words by Imogen Holst

Verse 2:
Wise men came from far, and saw him
Knelt in homage to adore him
Precious gifts they laid before him
Gold and frankincense and myrrh.

Verse 3:
Let us now in every nation
Sing his praise with exultation
All the world shall find salvation
In the birth of Mary's Son.

Sans Day Carol

Traditional

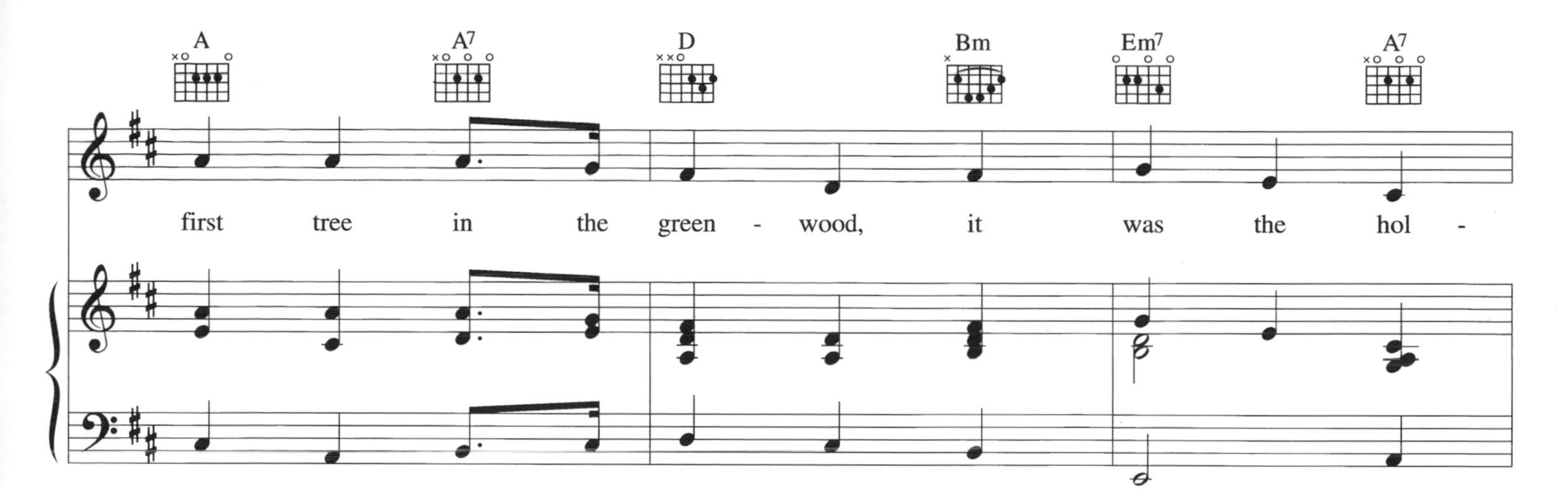

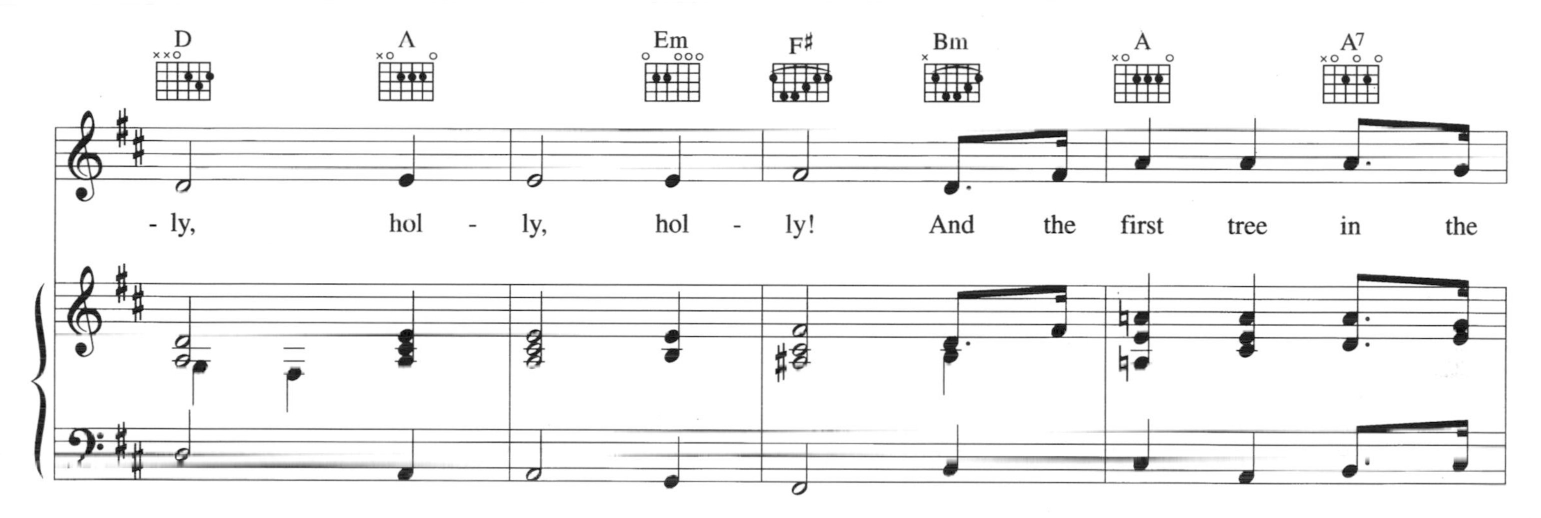

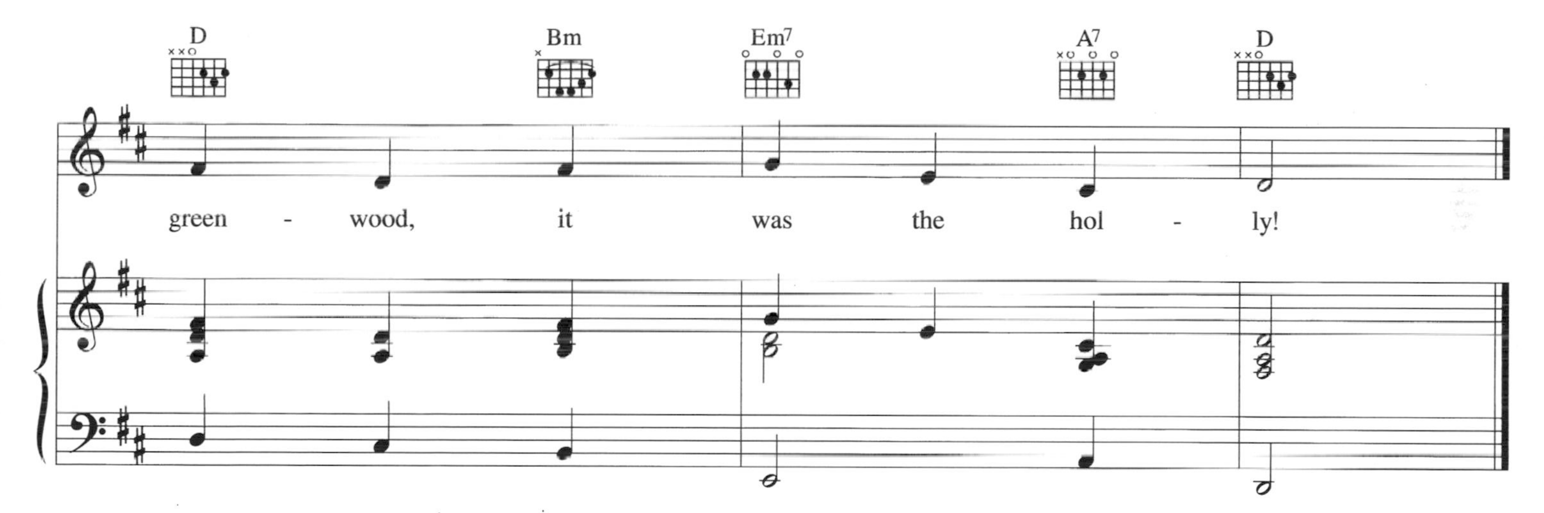

Verse 2:
Now the holly bears a berry
As green as the grass
And Mary bore Jesus
Who died on the cross.

And Mary bore Jesus Christ etc.

Verse 3:
Now the holly bears a berry
As black as the coal
And Mary bore Jesus
Who died for us all.

And Mary bore Jesus Christ etc.

Verse 4:
Now the holly bears a berry
As blood is it red
Then trust we our Saviour
Who rose from the dead.

And Mary bore Jesus Christ etc.

See Amid The Winter's Snow

Words by Edward Caswall
Music by John Goss

Verse 2:
Lo, within a manger lies
He who built the starry skies
He who, throned in height sublime
Sits amid the Cherubim.

Hail, thou ever-blessed morn! *etc.*

Verse 3:
Say, ye holy shepherds, say
What your joyful news today?
Wherefore have ye left your sheep
On the lonely mountain steep?

Hail, thou ever-blessed morn! *etc.*

Verse 4:
'As we watched at dead of night
Lo! we saw a wonderous light
Angels singing "Peace on earth"
Told us of the Saviour's birth'.

Hail, thou ever-blessed morn! *etc.*

Verse 5:
Sacred Infant, all-divine
What a tender love was thine
Thus to come from highest bliss
Down to such a world as this!

Hail, thou ever-blessed morn! *etc.*

Verse 6:
Teach, O teach us, Holy Child
By thy face so meek and mild
Teach us to resemble thee
In thy sweet humility!

Hail, thou ever-blessed morn! *etc.*

Silent Night

Words by Joseph Mohr
Music by Franz Gruber

2. Silent night! Holy night!
   Shepherds quake at the sight!
   Glories stream from Heaven afar
   Heav'nly hosts sing Alleluia
   Christ, the Saviour, is born!
   Christ, the Saviour, is born!

3. Silent night! Holy night!
   Son of God, love's pure light
   Radiant beams from Thy holy face
   With the dawn of redeeming grace
   Jesus, Lord, at Thy birth
   Jesus, Lord, at Thy birth.

Sing Lullaby

Music: Traditional
Words by Sabine Baring-Gould

Verse 2:
Sing lullaby!
Lullaby baby, now a-sleeping
Sing lullaby!
Hush! do not wake the infant King
Soon will come sorrow with the morning
Soon will come bitter grief and weeping
Sing lullaby!

Verse 3:
Sing lullaby!
Lullaby baby, now a-dozing
Sing lullaby!
Hush! do not wake the infant King
Soon comes the Cross, the nails, the piercing
Then in the grave at last reposing
Sing lullaby!

Verse 4:
Sing lullaby!
Lullaby! is the Babe awaking?
Sing lullaby!
Hush! do not stir the infant King
Dreaming of Easter, gladsome morning
Conquering death, its bondage breaking
Sing lullaby!

Sussex Carol

Traditional

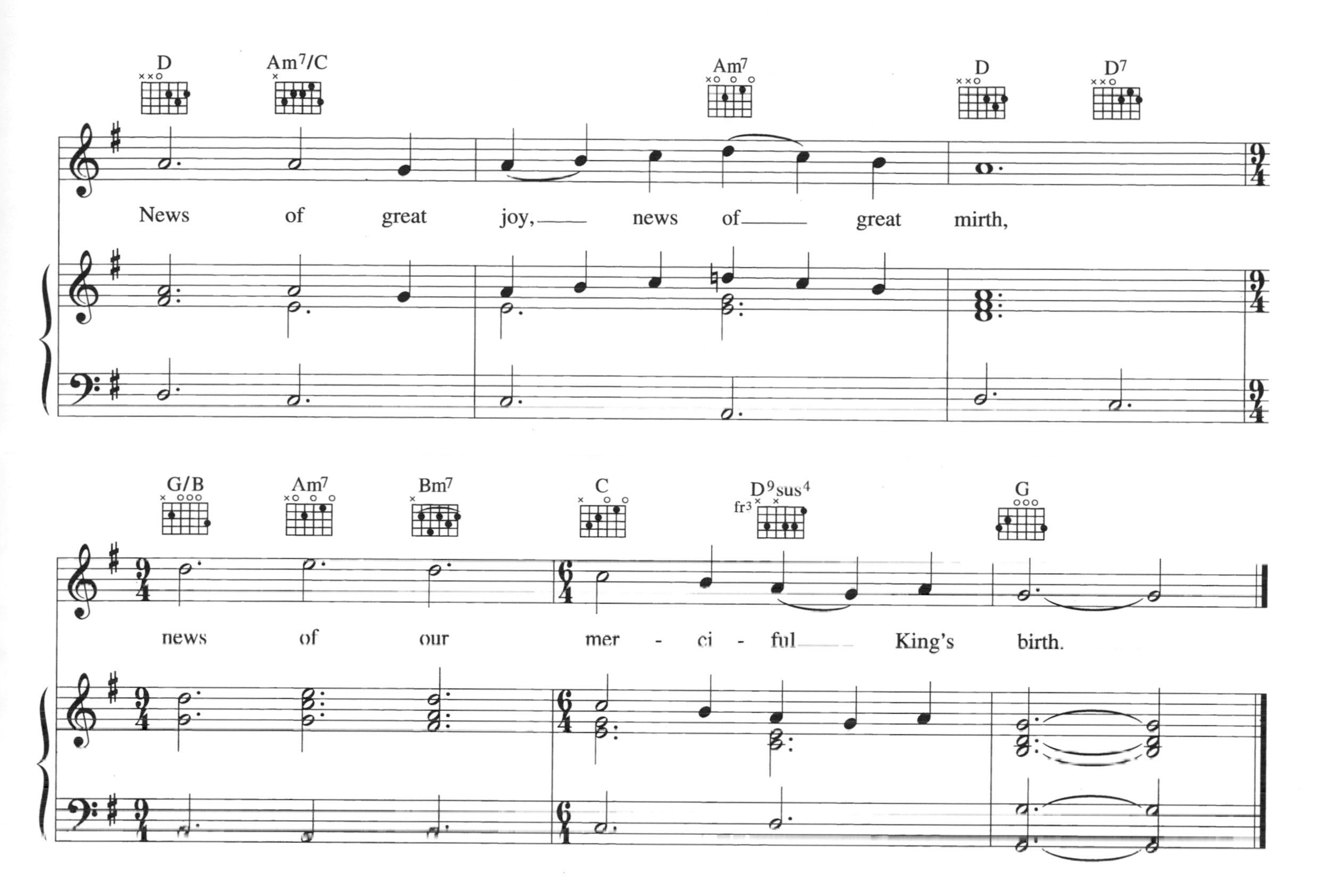

Verse 2:
Then why should men on earth be so sad
Since our Redeemer made us glad
Then why should men on earth be so sad
Since our Redeemer made us glad
When from our sin he set us free
All for to gain our liberty?

Verse 3:
When sin departs before his grace
Then life and health come in its place
When sin departs before his grace
Then life and health come in its place
Angels and men with joy may sing
All for to see the newborn King.

Verse 4:
All out of darkness we have light
Which made the angels sing this night
All out of darkness we have light
Which made the angels sing this night
"Glory to God and peace to men
Now and for evermore. Amen."

The Truth From Above

Traditional

Verse 2:
The first thing which I do relate
Is that God did man create
The next thing which to you I'll tell
Woman was made with man to dwell.

Verse 3:
Thus we were heirs to endless woes
Till God the Lord did interpose
And so a promise soon did run
That he would redeem us by his Son.

Verse 4:
And at that season of the year
Our blest Redeemer did appear
He here did live, and here did preach
And many thousands he did teach.

Verse 5:
Thus he in love to us behaved
To show us how we must be saved
And if you want to know the way
Be pleased to hear what he did say.

The Twelve Days Of Christmas

Traditional

F
B♭
F
Dm
Gm
fr3
C
F
tree. 3. On the third day of Christ - mas, my true love gave to me

C
Gm7
fr3
C7
F
B♭
F
C7
Three French_ hens, Two tur - tle doves and a par - tridge_ in a pear

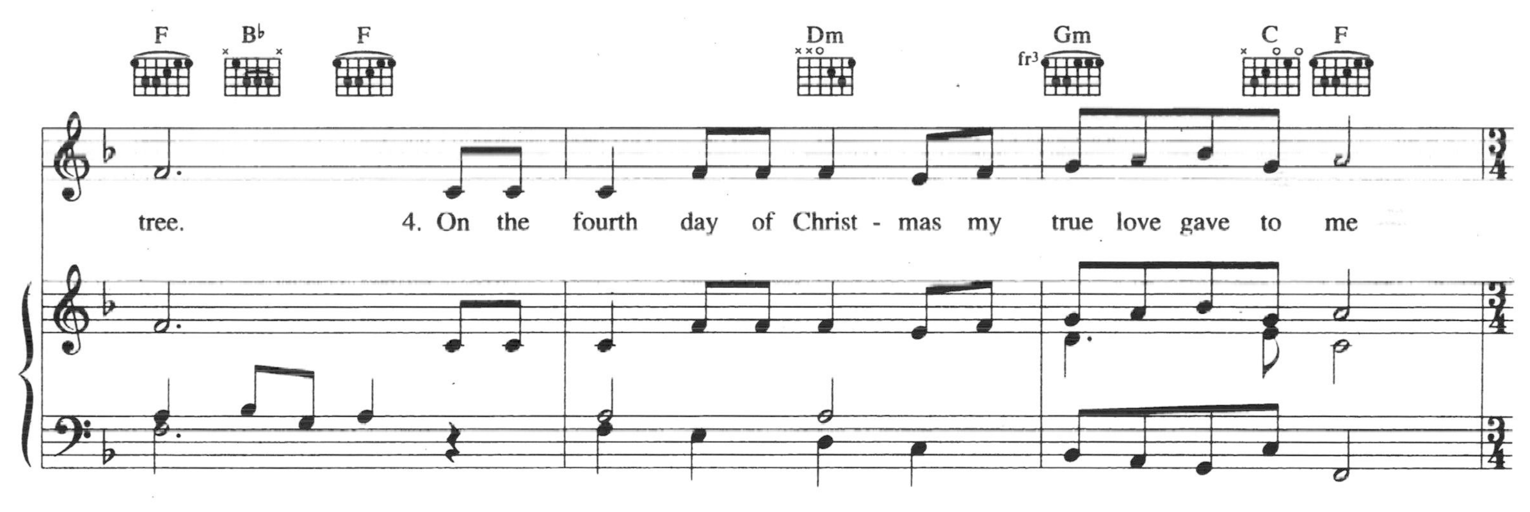
F
B♭
F
Dm
Gm
fr3
C
F
tree. 4. On the fourth day of Christ - mas my true love gave to me

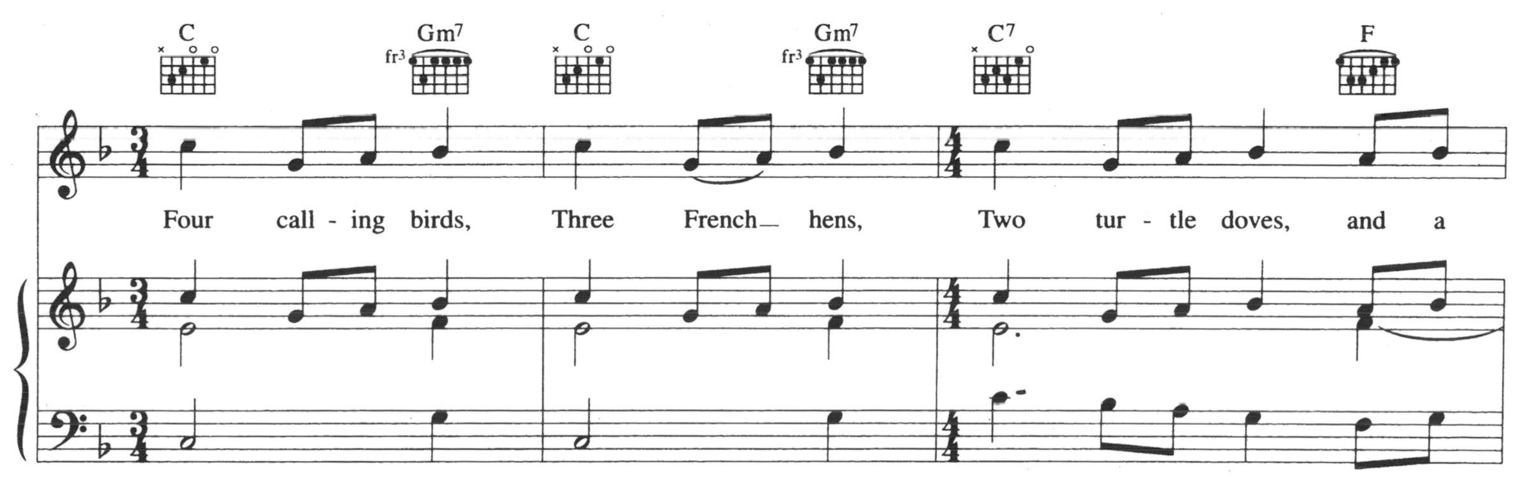
C
Gm7
fr3
C
Gm7
fr3
C7
F
Four call - ing birds, Three French_ hens, Two tur - tle doves, and a

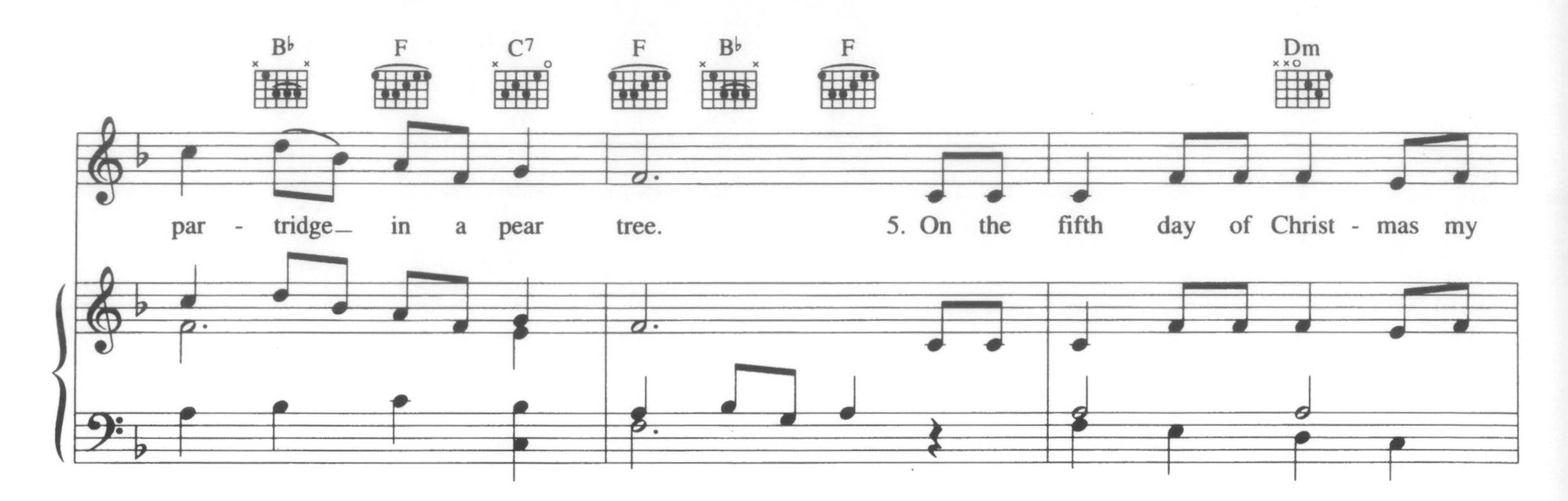
B♭ F C7 F B♭ F Dm
par - tridge in a pear tree. 5. On the fifth day of Christ - mas my

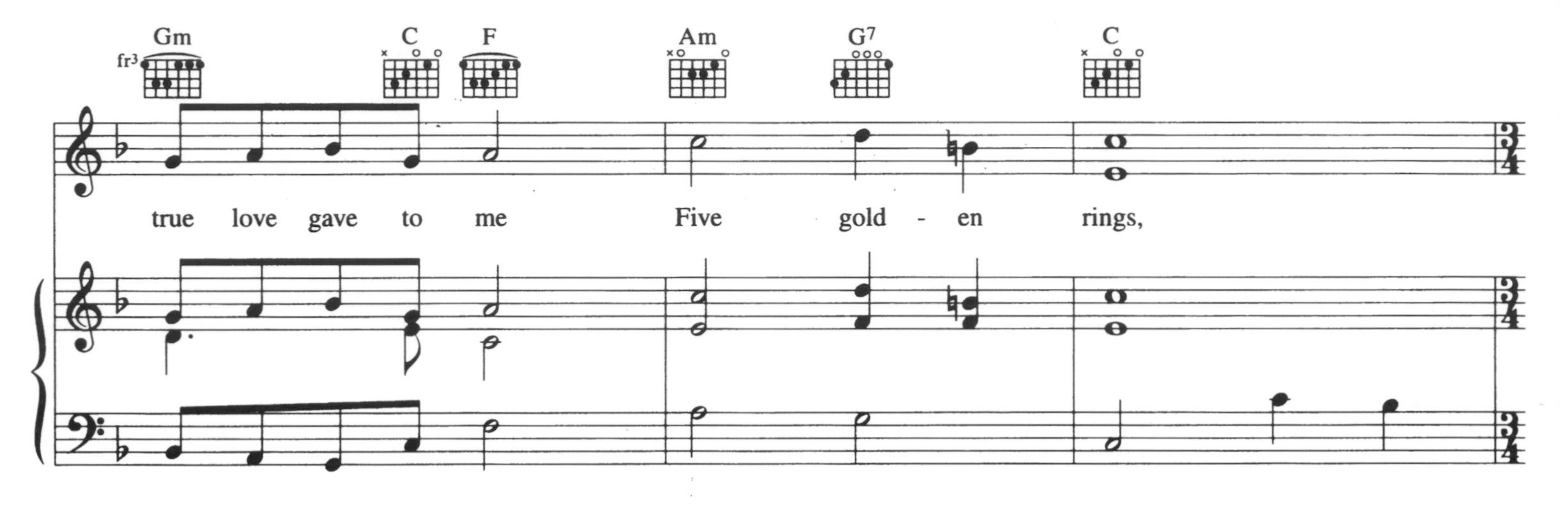
Gm fr3 C F Am G7 C
true love gave to me Five gold - en rings,

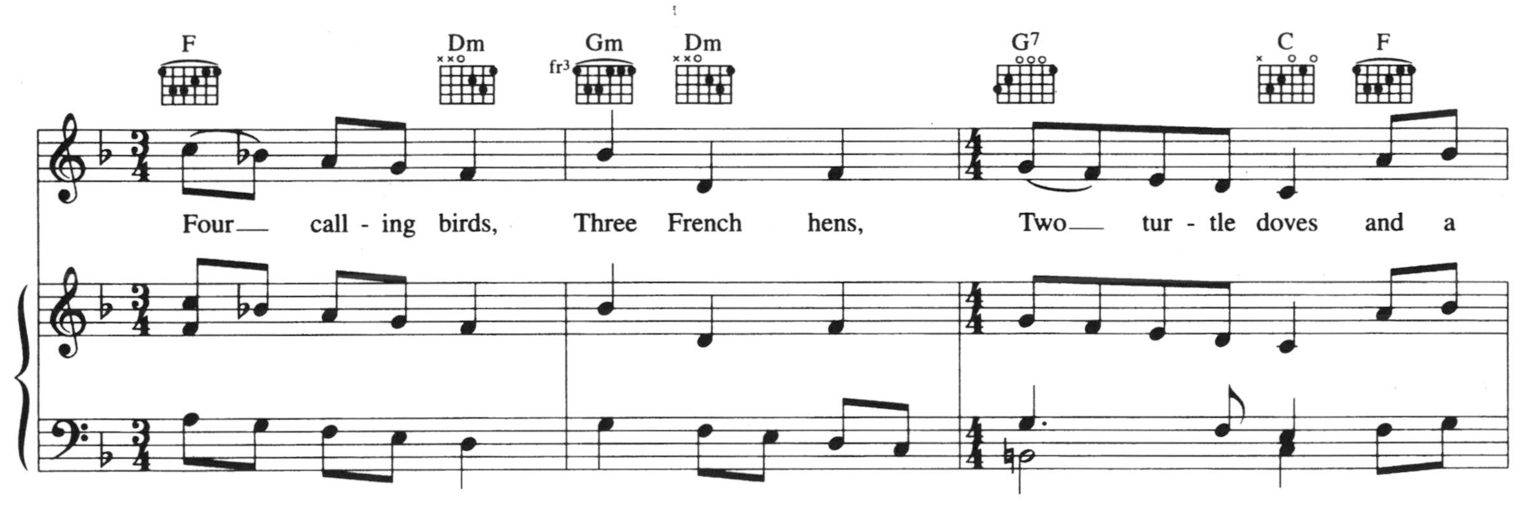
F Dm Gm fr3 Dm G7 C F
Four call - ing birds, Three French hens, Two tur - tle doves and a

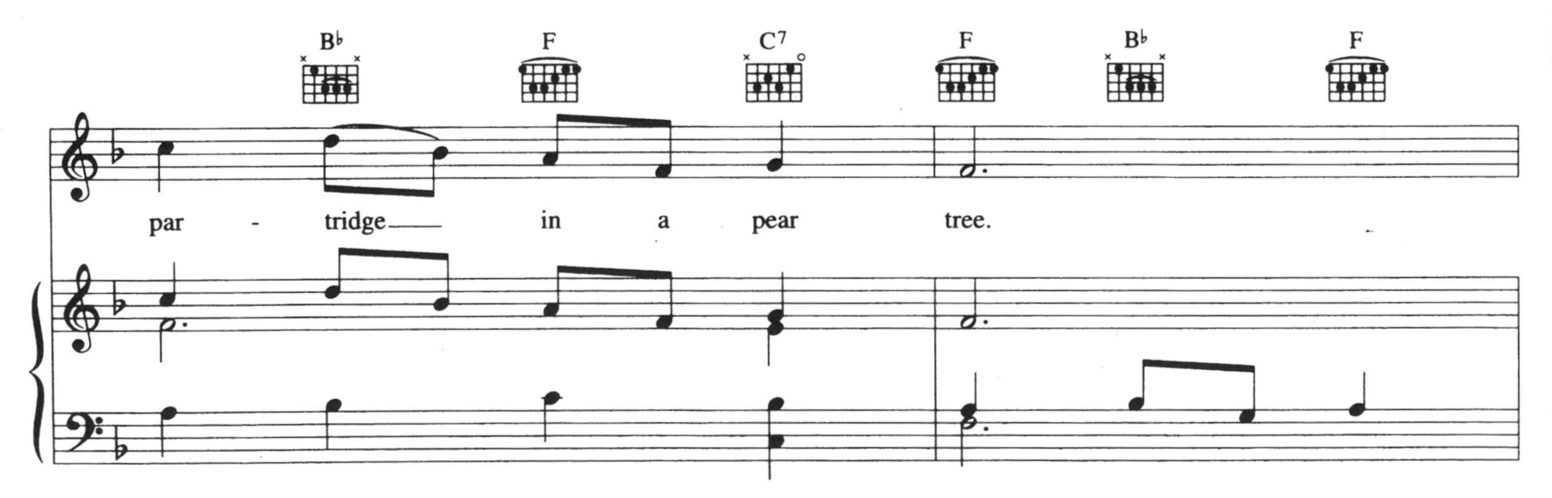
B♭ F C7 F B♭ F
par - tridge in a pear tree.

F Dm C F C Gm7
fr3
6. On the sixth day of Christ - mas my true love gave to me Six geese a - lay - ing,
7. On the seventh day of Christ - mas my true love gave to me Sev - en swans a - swim-ming,
8. On the eighth day of Christ - mas my true love gave to me Eight maids a - milk - ing,
9. On the ninth day of Christ - mas my true love gave to me Nine la - dies wait - ing,
10. On the tenth day of Christ - mas my true love gave to me Ten lords a - leap - ing,
11. On the eleventh day of Christ - mas my true love gave to me 'Lev - en pip - ers pip - ing,
12. On the twelfth day of Christ - mas my true love gave to me Twelve drum-mers drum-mimg,
* Repeat this measure as often as necessary, so that these lines may be sung in reverse order, each time ending with "Six geese a-laying."
Am G7 C F Dm Gm Dm
Five gold - en rings, Four— call - ing birds, Three French hens,
6-11. D.𝄋 12. rit.
G7 C F B♭ F C7 F B♭ F F B♭ F
Two— tur - tle doves, and a par - tridge— in a pear tree. tree.

Rocking

Traditional Czech Carol

Unto Us A Boy Is Born

Traditional
English Words by George Woodward

Verse 2:
Cradled in a stall was He
With sleepy cows and asses
But the very beasts could see
That He all men surpasses.

Verse 3:
Herod then with fear was filled
"A prince", he said, "in Jewry!"
All the little boys he killed
At Bethlem in his fury.

Verse 4:
Now may Mary's son, who came
So long ago to love us
Lead us all with hearts aflame
Unto the joys above us.

Verse 5:
Omega and Alpha he!
Let the organ thunder
While the choir with peals of glee
Doth rend the air asunder.

Wassail Song

Traditional

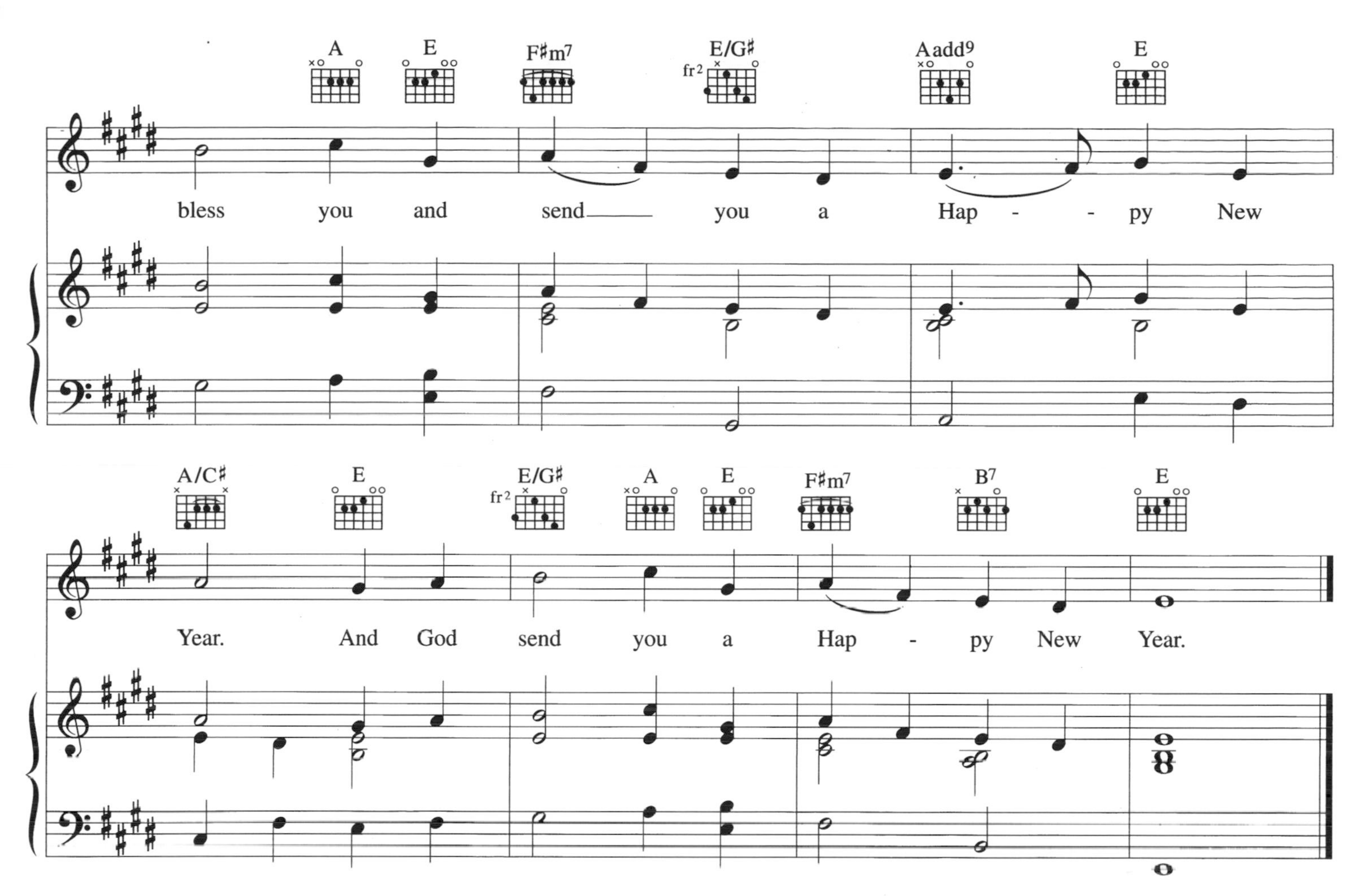

Verse 2:
Our wassail cup is made
Of the rosemary tree
And so is your beer
Of the best barley:

Love and joy come to you *etc.*

Verse 3:
We are not daily beggars
That beg from door to door
But we are neighbours' children
Whom you have seen before:

Love and joy come to you *etc.*

Verse 4:
Call up the butler of this house
Put on his golden ring
Let him bring us up a glass of beer
And better we shall sing.

Love and joy come to you *etc.*

Verse 5:
We have got a little purse
Of stretching leather skin
We want a little of your money
To line it well within:

Love and joy come to you *etc.*

Verse 6:
Bring us out a table
And spread it with a cloth
Bring us out a mouldy cheese
And some of your Christmas loaf:

Love and joy come to you *etc.*

Verse 7:
God bless the master of this house
Likewise the mistress too
And all the little children
That round the table go:

Love and joy come to you *etc.*

Verse 8:
Good master and good mistress
While you're sitting by the fire
Pray think of us poor children
Who are wand'ring in the mire.

Love and joy come to you *etc.*

We Three Kings Of Orient Are

Words & Music by John Henry Hopkins

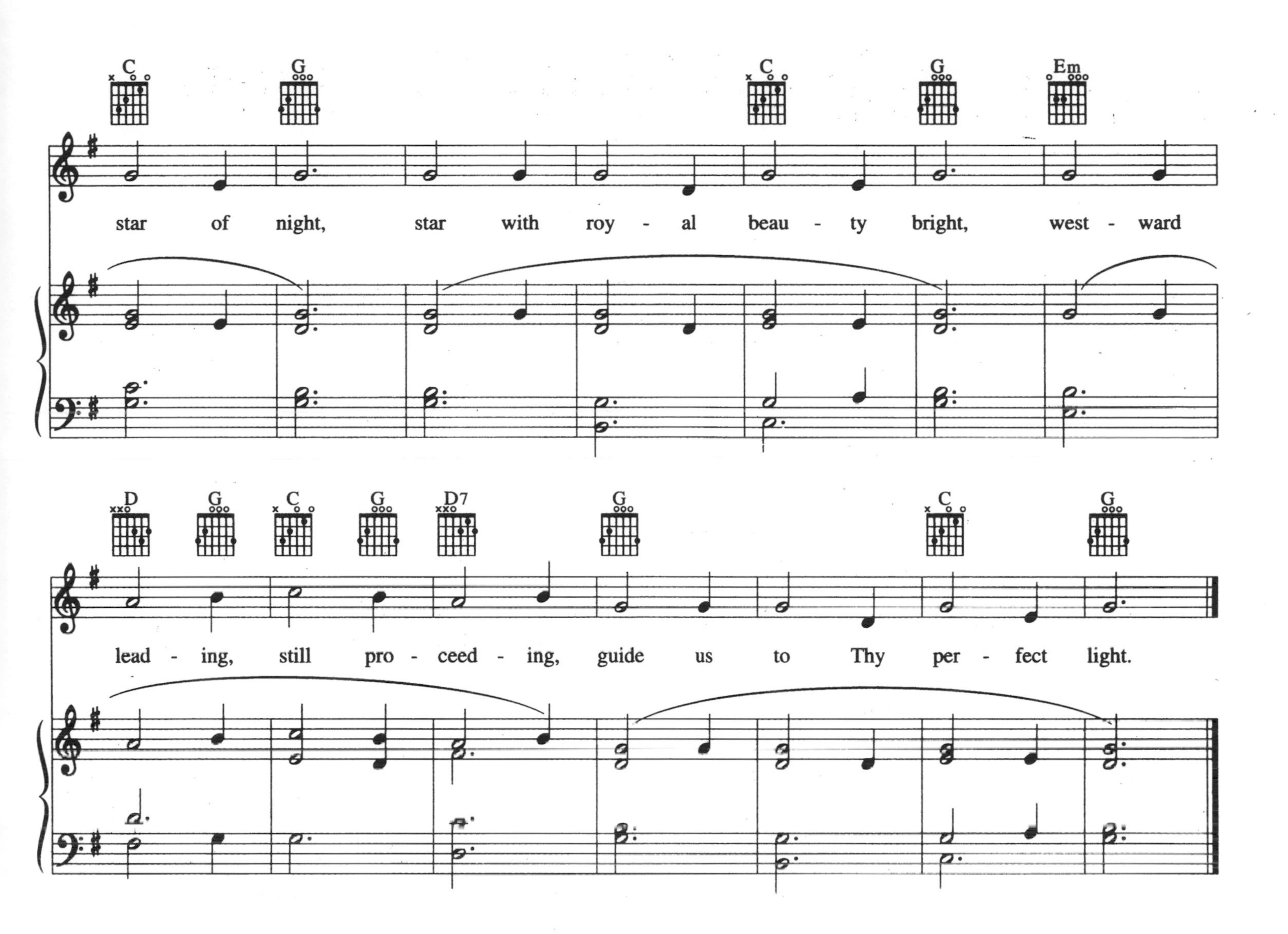

2. Born a King on Bethlehem plain
Gold I bring to crown Him again
King forever, ceasing never
Over us all to reign.
Refrain

3. Frankincense to offer have I
Incense owns a Deity night
Prayer and praising, all men raising
Worship Him, God on high.
Refrain

4. Myrrh is mine; its bitter perfume
Breathes a life of gathering gloom
Sorrowing, sighing, bleeding, dying
Sealed in the stone cold tomb.
Refrain

5. Glorious now behold Him arise
King and God, and sacrifice
Heaven sings Alleluia
Alleluia the earth replies
Refrain

We Wish You A Merry Christmas

Traditional

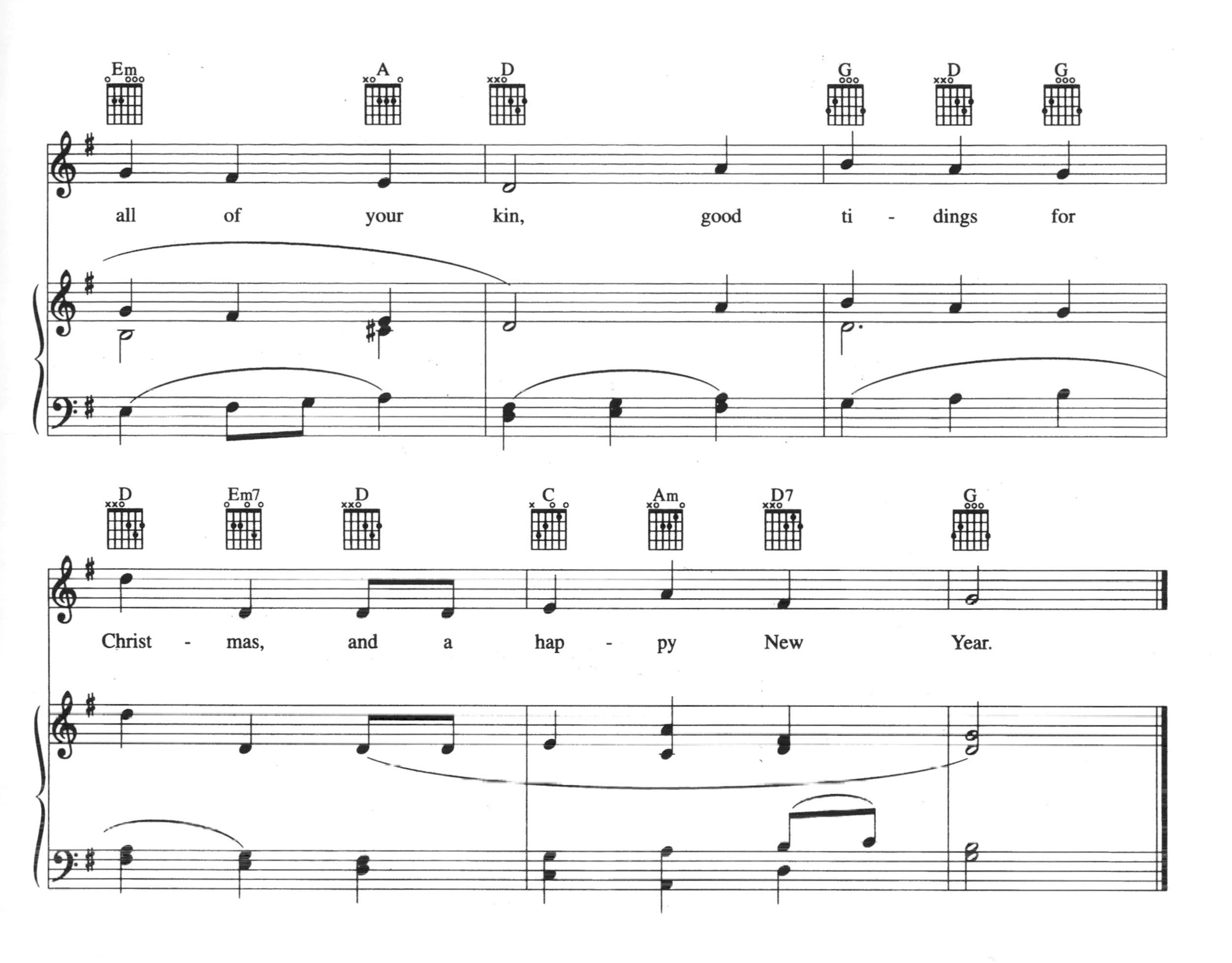

2. Oh, bring us some figgy pudding
   Oh, bring us some figgy pudding
   Oh, bring us some figgy pudding
   And bring it out here!
   Refrain

3. We won't go until we got some
   We won't go until we got some
   We won't go until we got some
   So bring some out here.
   Refrain

What Child Is This

Music: Traditional
Words by William Chatterton Dix

Verse 2:
Why lies he in such mean estate
Where ox and ass are feeding?
Good Christians, fear: for sinners here
The silent Word is pleading.
Nails, spear, shall pierce him through
The cross be borne for me, for you
Hail, hail the Word made flesh
The Babe, the Son of Mary!

Verse 3:
So bring him incense, gold and myrrh
Come rich and poor, to own him.
The King of kings salvation brings
Let loving hearts enthrone him.
Raise, raise the song on high
The Virgin sings her lullaby
Joy, joy for Christ is born
The Babe, the Son of Mary!

Whence Is That Goodly Fragrance

Traditional

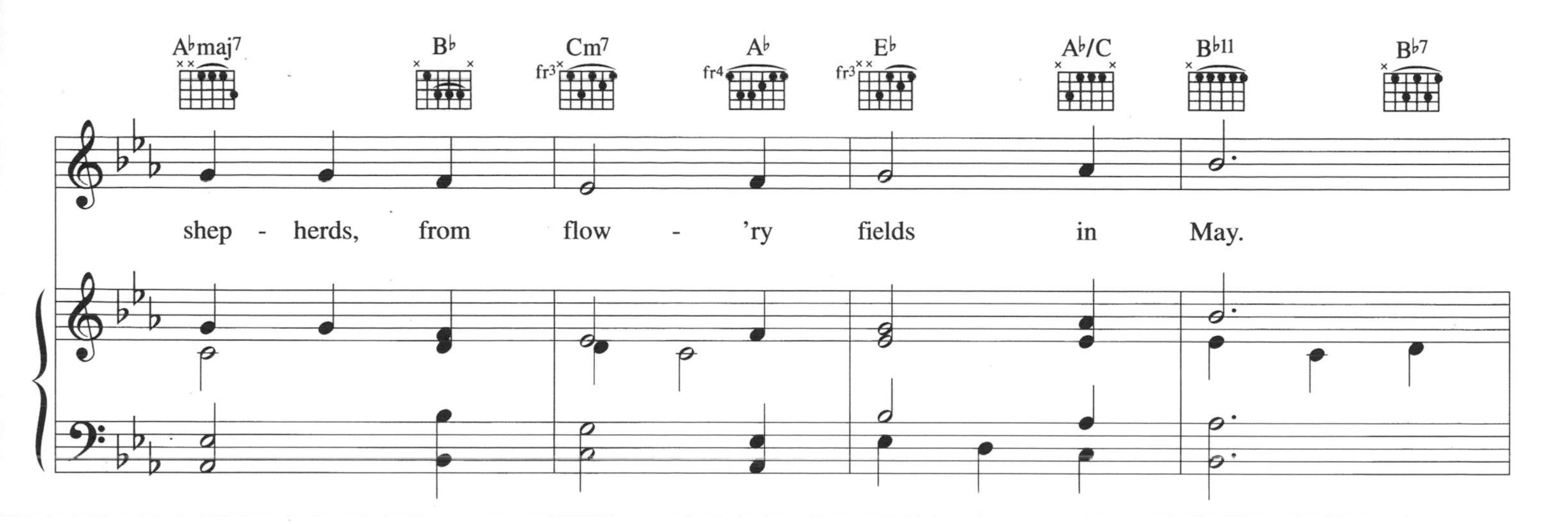

Verse 2:
What is that light so brilliant, breaking
Here in the night across our eyes?
Never so bright the day-star waking
Started to climb the morning skies!
What is that light so brilliant, breaking
Here in the night across our eyes?

Verse 3:
Bethlehem! there in manger lying
Find your Redeemer, haste away!
Run ye with eager footsteps hieing!
Worship the Saviour born to-day!
Bethlehem! there in manger lying
Find your Redeemer, haste away!

While Shepherds Watched

Music: Traditional
Words by Nahum Tate

2. "Fear not!" said He, for mighty dread
Had seized their troubled mind
"Glad tidings of great joy I bring
To you and all mankind."

3. "To you, in David's town, this day
Is born of David's line
The Saviour who is Christ the Lord
And this shall be the sign."

4. "The Heav'nly Babe you there shall find
To human view displayed
All meanly wrapped in swathing bands
And in a manger laid."

5. "All glory be to God on high
And to the earth be peace
Good will henceforth from heav'n to men
Begin and never cease."